D0991981

The Death of Adolf Hitler
Unknown Documents from Soviet Archives

The Death of
Adolf Hitler

■

Unknown Documents from Soviet Archives

Lev Bezymenski

MICHAEL JOSEPH
LONDON

First published in Great Britain by

Michael Joseph Ltd

26 Bloomsbury Street,

London WC1

1968

© 1968 by Christian Wegner Verlag, Hamburg

English translation © 1968 by Harcourt, Brace & World, Inc.

Originally published in Germany under the title

Der Tod des Adolf Hitler

Printed lithographically in Great Britain

by the Hollen Street Press at Slough

7181   0634   2

Thanks are due to the following for permission to reproduce
material in which they hold the copyright
Odhams Press, London: Hitler, A Study in Tyranny by Alan Bullock
Hutchinson Ltd, London: Kersten: Memoirs 1940-1945

Note about the Author

Lev Bezymenski was born in 1920 in Kazan, the son of the poet Alexander Bezymenski. He studied philosophy in Moscow, and in 1941 entered the Soviet Armed Forces, serving first as a private and later as an officer, in Stalingrad, Kursk, and Berlin. An excellent scholar of German, he served as interpreter at the hearings of General Paulus, the German Field Marshal who surrendered to the Russians after the battle of Stalingrad. As member of Marshal Zhukov's staff, he participated in the battle of Berlin.

In 1946 he became co-editor of Novoe Vremia, a foreign-affairs journal. In this capacity he made various trips abroad, producing numerous articles on current events which were published throughout the Eastern countries.

Contents

Illustrations

The Death of Adolf Hitler
Unknown Documents from Soviet Archives

1

Nearly a quarter of a century has gone by since the end of
World War II, yet not all its enigmas have been solved. War—
any war—poses a number of questions, of greater or less importance. Here we are concerned with World War II and particularly with the circumstances of its end, with an enigma that
pertains to the final days preceding the cessation of fighting. An
enigma that might be considered not worth bothering about,
since it concerns the death of a single man. Why, one may ask,
give so much importance to an individual, when so many millions of unknown soldiers and civilians, most of them innocent,
perished?

The toll taken by the adventure of Nazism of the German
people alone was tremendous. Official West German statistics
record 4,192,000 German war dead; American estimates go up
to 9 million. Soviet historians, basing themselves on German
documents that fell into Russian hands, arrive at a similar
figure: 9 million dead (not including the victims among the
civilian population). Be that as it may, in terms of quantity we
are concerned in this text with a single person only, and his
death. But this person, Adolf Hitler, was the cause of the
annihilation of those millions.

Many responsible authors of historical works and many irresponsible authors of sensational articles in illustrated magazines have devoted much attention to the last days and hours of "War Criminal Number One." But they have confused the issue rather than clarifying it.

William Shirer, in his by now classic work on the Third Reich, writes toward the end:

The bones were never found, and this gave rise to rumors after the war that Hitler had survived. But the separate interrogation of several eyewitnesses by British and American intelligence officers leaves no doubt about the matter. Kempka has given a plausible explanation as to why the charred bones were never found. "The traces were wiped out," he told his interrogators, "by the uninterrupted Russian artillery fire." [1]

The Englishman Alan Bullock, in his comprehensive biography of Hitler, writes:

What happened to the ashes of the two burned bodies left in the Chancellery Garden has never been discovered. That they were disposed of in some way remains a possibility, since an open fire will not normally destroy the human body so completely as to leave no traces, and nothing was found in the garden after its capture by the Russians. Professor Trevor-Roper, who carried out a thorough investigation in 1945 of the circumstances surrounding Hitler's death, inclines to the view that the ashes were collected into a box and handed to Artur Axmann, the leader of the Hitler Youth. There is some slight evidence for this and, as Trevor-Roper points out (in the Introduction to his second edition, pages xxxii-xxxiv), it would have been a logical act to pass on the sacred relics to the next generation. The simplest explanation may still be

[1] William Shirer, *The Rise and Fall of the Third Reich* (New York, 1959), p. 1134.

4

the correct one. It is not known how thorough a search was made by the Russians, and it is possible that the remains of Adolf Hitler and his wife became mixed up with those of other bodies which have been found there, especially as the garden continued to be under bombardment until the Russians captured the Chancellery on 2 May.

The question would scarcely be of interest had the failure to discover the remains not been used to throw doubt on the fact of Hitler's death. It is, of course, true that no final incontrovertible evidence in the form of Hitler's dead body has been produced.[2]

But what researcher, what journalist in our century of documentation would let matters rest there, as long as the last incontrovertible piece of evidence has not been found? The German journalist Erich Kuby went to Moscow to search for the remains of the "Führer," thinking that they might lie, mummified, in a lead coffin, or be preserved in alcohol. He comforted himself with the tiny hope: "Moscow's mills, as we know, grind slowly. One day we will surely be able to read the verbatim text of the autopsy report, will come to know where the corpses of Hitler and his wife ended up." [3]

Let us now turn these Moscow millstones.

2

The Gospels according to the twentieth century have in their beginning not the Word, but the document. Hence we begin our tale with an official protocol set down and signed in May 1945, in Berlin, by an officer and three soldiers of the Red Army.

[2] Alan Bullock, *Hitler, A Study in Tyranny,* revised edition (London, 1962), p. 800.
[3] Erich Kuby, *Die Russen in Berlin* (Munich, 1965), p. 303.

REPORT

Berlin, Field Army
1945, May, fifth day

I, Lieutenant of the Guards Panassov, Alexei Alexandrovich, and privates Churakov, Ivan Dimitrievich, Oleynik, Yevgeni Stepanovich, and Serukh, Ilya Yefremovich, found in the city of Berlin on the grounds of Hitler's Chancellery, next to the spot where the corpses of Goebbels and his wife were discovered, and close to Hitler's private [1] bunker two corpses (the corpse of a woman and of a man) and took them in custody.

The corpses were severely charred by fire and it is impossible to identify them without additional information.

The corpses are being held in Counter Intelligence Section SMERSH,[2] 79th Rifle Corps.

Platoon Commander, Counter Intelligence Section SMERSH, 79th RC.
Lieutenant of the Guards
signed (Panassov)

Private, Counter Intelligence Section SMERSH, 79th RC.
signed (Churakov)

Private, Counter Intelligence Section SMERSH, 79th RC.
signed (Oleynik)

Private, Counter Intelligence Section SMERSH, 79th RC.
signed (Serukh)

It took roughly four years of shelling and fighting along fronts extended over 1000 km. for Ivan Churakov to report this discovery and for Lieutenant Alexei Panassov with his soldiers to draw up this document. Justice almost always triumphs, but never automatically. The soldier Ivan—as we shall hear subse-

---

[1] Inserted by hand.
[2] SMERSH—abbreviation for the Counter Intelligence Service in the Soviet Union during the War ("Death to Spies!").

6

quently, it was he who was the first to discover the corpses—did not know at the time whose corpses he had found, nor did Lieutenant Panassov know that his report would become part of the history of World War II.

For this very reason, a description of the circumstances that brought Ivan Churakov to Berlin seems called for.

3

The encirclement and conquest of Berlin were the logical end result of an operation which had been prepared and initiated in STAVKA (the general headquarters of the Red Army) in the spring of 1945. At the time, Adolf Hitler still hoped that Soviet troops would not march on Berlin. As late as March of that year he said to his Chief of Staff, General (*Generaloberst*) Heinz Guderian: "The Russians won't be as stupid as we were when we let ourselves be tempted by Moscow's proximity and tried to take the capital at all costs. It was you, Guderian, who wanted to be the first to enter Moscow at the head of your army! You should know best the epilogue to the matter!" [1]

Guderian did indeed know the epilogue to this attack. What began in Moscow ended in Berlin. But in fact Hitler tried to convince himself and those around him that the German capital would be spared the annihilating impact of the Red Army. Not only Hitler but his military advisers were in need of this "self-therapy." Generals A. Philippi and R. Heim later confirmed that German Counter Intelligence had learned by mid-March of dissensions in the Soviet Supreme Command concerning the deployment of operations: Marshal Zhukov was said to be in favor of attacking Berlin directly, while Stalin favored an attack on Prague. . . .[2]

---

[1] This quotation is not found in Guderian's Memoirs—no general likes to be reminded of his failures. But Hitler's words were stored in the memory of a bystander, of whom we shall hear more later on.
[2] Cf. *Der Feldzug gegen Sowjetrussland* (Stuttgart, 1962), p. 284.

When I asked Marshal Chuikov about this, he burst out laughing: "Nonsense! In this case, as in others, the Germans did not know what our intentions were. At that moment Operation Berlin was not just on the planning board but was organized down to the last detail. . . ."

The battle for Berlin had been in careful preparation for some time. By the beginning of February the troops of the 1st Byelorussian Front had reached the Oder near Küstrin. In various memoirs we find the opinion that, with greater boldness, the Soviet troops might have taken Berlin even then in a surprise action.[3] Zhukov, then Commander-in-Chief of the 1st Byelorussian Front, comments: "To overrate the capacities of one's own forces is just as dangerous as to underestimate the forces of the enemy. . . ." Accordingly, he allowed himself two months' time for the preparation of the final battle.

Every Soviet officer and soldier who fought during those exciting days with the 1st Byelorussian or the 1st Ukrainian Front knows the importance of the battle of Berlin. The same may be said of the soldiers of the German 9th Army and the 3rd Panzer Corps. Only Mr. Cornelius Ryan, author of the American bestseller *The Last Battle,* seems unaware of it. He follows the old journalistic rule according to which no one would be surprised if a reporter said that a man had been bitten by a dog, but that this same reporter would make a lot of money with the story that a dog had been bitten by a man. Mr. Ryan no doubt thought that he would elicit no surprise by describing a battle for Berlin, but that he would find general attention if it was learned that that battle never took place. His version is the preferred one of all those who wish to prove that the strategic capacity of Soviet marshals isn't really so great, compared with the achievements of the defenders of Berlin or the strategic

[3] Soviet generals and historians analyzed extensively a similar thesis advanced some years ago by Marshal V. I. Chuikov, who thought that the march on Berlin might have been undertaken as early as January 1945. But the consensus is that Soviet troops had no real chance for a successful attack on Berlin at that time, and no such proposals were considered by the Supreme Command.

8

capacities of American generals who would have found it easy to conquer that last citadel of the dying German Reich.[4]

The battle for Berlin was one of the mightiest in military history. Three Soviet Fronts and two German armies were involved. From April 16 to May 2, the din of battle did not stop a single day. The German Armed Forces refused to capitulate, though they might have saved the lives of several hundred thousands of Germans. But what did hundreds of thousands matter to Hitler, who was responsible for the annihilation of many million human lives?

4

It would be senseless exaggeration to say that the Soviet Army battled for Berlin merely because Adolf Hitler was there. It had other, more important goals. This may explain why Soviet historical writing has so far paid little attention to Hitler's final fate.

But it was only natural that, simultaneously with the attack on Berlin, the question was raised of where War Criminal Number One might be. The situation was not as clear then as it appears now, to our hindsight. In Moscow one did not trust the news releases in the official Nazi press. The Military Command of the Soviet Union did not possess any precise information as to Hitler's whereabouts at the time of the offensive. Fairly reliable proofs of his presence in the capital of the Reich became available only about April 20. The celebrations on the occasion of his fifty-sixth birthday—on which day Hitler left his bunker for the last time—confirmed the news in the Nazi press, but there was no guarantee that he would stay on in Berlin.

Historians have the inestimable advantage over eyewitnesses of being able to see behind the scenes of both fronts. Those officers of the 1st Byelorussian Front who were charged with

---

[4] This ludicrous stand brings to mind the Russian proverb: "Once the fight is finished, one doesn't raise fists!" Harry Hopkins, Roosevelt's closest adviser, openly admitted at the time: "We would have taken Berlin if we had been able to do so."

the search for the chief war criminal, had no idea of what was happening in the Führer's bunker. The historian, however, can consult his sources, among them the so far unpublished, valuable report of SS-Sturmbannführer Otto Günsche. This active member of the SS, one of the officers of the "Leibstandarte Adolf Hitler," Hitler's bodyguard, personal adjutant of the Führer in the years 1943 and 1944, was not by nature a writer of memoirs. But Günsche had to spend an extended period in Soviet prisons and there was encouraged to write a book or, more precisely, dictate it to his interrogators. His depositions were immediately translated and put on record. Another well-informed eyewitness, SS-Sturmbannführer Heinz Linge, Hitler's valet from 1935 to 1945, was called upon to complete Günsche's story. Here is what he had to say: [1]

On April 21 Hitler was roused at about 9:30 A.M. and informed that Berlin was in the line of fire of Russian artillery. Burgdorf [2] as well as other adjutants waited for him in the antechamber. Ten minutes later Hitler, unshaven, hastily entered the antechamber. As a rule he did his own shaving. Not even his personal barber, August Wollenhaupt, was allowed to shave him; he said that he could not bear to have anyone with a razor operate close to his throat.

In the antechamber, the following waited for Hitler: Burgdorf, Schaub,[3] Below,[4] and Günsche.

"What is happening? Where is the shooting coming from?" he asked. Burgdorf reported that the center of Berlin was under heavy artillery fire from a Russian battery, positioned apparently northwest of Zossen. Hitler blanched. "Are the Russians that close?"

On April 22 early in the morning the fire from the Russian artillery increased. . . . Russian shells burst frequently in the

[1] Translated from the Russian.
[2] General Wilhelm Burgdorf, Hitler's adjutant-in-chief, Chief of Army Personnel.
[3] Julius Schaub, Hitler's personal adjutant.
[4] Colonel Nicolaus von Below, Air Force adjutant.

Tiergarten and occasionally even in the gardens surrounding the ministries on Wilhelmstrasse. Their thunder tore Hitler from sleep at nine in the morning.

As soon as he was dressed he called Linge and asked excitedly: "What caliber?" To calm Hitler, Linge answered that the fire came from anti-aircraft batteries in the Tiergarten and from isolated Russian long-range guns. After breakfast in his study Hitler went back to his bedroom, where Morell [5] gave him the usual pep injection.

The military conference was called for 12 o'clock noon. Around noon, the following gathered in Hitler's bunker: Doenitz,[6] Keitel,[7] Jodl,[8] Krebs,[9] Burgdorf, Winter,[10] Christian,[11] Voss, Fegelein,[12] Bormann,[13] Hewel,[14] Lorenz,[15] Below, Günsche, Johannmeier,[16] John von Freyend,[17] and von Freitag-Loringhoven.[18]

It was the shortest military conference of the entire war. Many of the faces were distorted. In muffled voices, the same question was repeated over and over again: "Why can't the Führer make up his mind to leave Berlin?"

Hitler came from his private rooms, his stoop seeming more pronounced than ever. He greeted the members of the conference laconically and dropped into a chair. Krebs started

[5] Theodor Morell, Hitler's private physician.
[6] This must be an error. Doenitz had left Berlin early that morning. He left behind as his deputy, Vice-Admiral Hans-Erich Voss.
[7] Wilhelm Keitel, Field Marshal, Armed Forces Chief of High Command.
[8] Alfred Jodl, *Generaloberst,* Armed Forces Chief of Operations.
[9] Hans Krebs, General of the Infantry, Acting Chief of the Army General Staff.
[10] August Winter, Mountain Troops General, Jodl's deputy.
[11] Eckhard Christian, *Generalmajor,* Air Force Chief of Operations.
[12] Hermann Fegelein, SS-Gruppenführer, General of Waffen-SS, Himmler's liaison officer.
[13] Martin Bormann, Reich Leader.
[14] Walther Hewel, Ambassador, Reich Foreign Ministry delegate at Führer Headquarters.
[15] Heinz Lorenz, representative of the German Press Bureau (DNB).
[16] Willy Johannmeyer, Major, Hitler's military adjutant.
[17] Ernst John von Freyend, Major, military adjutant of General Jodl.
[18] Bernd Freiherr Freytag von Loringhoven, Adjutant of the Chief of Staff.

11

his recital of the facts. He reported a considerable worsening in the situation of the German troops defending Berlin. Russian tanks had succeeded in breaking through in the south via Zossen and in reaching the outskirts of Berlin. In the eastern and northern suburbs there was violent fighting. German troops positioned on the Oder south of Stettin were hopelessly trapped. Russian tanks had infiltrated through a gap in the front and had penetrated deep into the German defense positions.

Hitler got up and bent down over the table. He started to point to something on the map, his hands shaking. Suddenly he straightened up and threw his colored pencils onto the table. He drew a deep breath, his face became flushed, his eyes opened wide. He took a step back from the table and in a breaking voice shrieked: "That's the end! Under such circumstances I can't direct anything any more! The war is lost! But you are mistaken, gentlemen, if you think that I will leave Berlin! I'd rather put a bullet through my head!"

Everyone stared at him in horror. He barely lifted his hand. "Thank you, gentlemen!" Then he left the room.

Those who had participated in the conference froze. Was this the end? Günsche followed Hitler. From the conference room voices called after Hitler: "But, mein Führer . . ." "I beg you, mein Führer . . ." Günsche caught up with Hitler at the door of his study. Hitler stopped and screamed: "Get Goebbels on the phone!"

Goebbels was living in the air-raid shelter of his villa on Hermann-Göring Strasse. While Hitler and Goebbels talked over the telephone, the others, in a state of utter confusion and panic, burst into the antechamber. Bormann and Keitel rushed up to Günsche: "Where is the Führer? What else did he say?" Günsche told them that the Führer was on the telephone with Goebbels. They all talked at once and interrupted each other. Keitel excitedly waved his hands, Bormann seemed beside himself and repeated ceaselessly: "It's impossible, the Führer can't really want to shoot himself!" Keitel screamed:

"We have to stop the Führer!" The chaos was indescribable. Some poured themselves brandy from the bottle that stood on the table.

Around half past twelve Goebbels arrived in the antechamber, limping, in extreme agitation: "Where is the Führer?" He was immediately led into Hitler's study. The conference between Hitler and Goebbels lasted about ten minutes. As Goebbels came out of the room, Bormann, Keitel, Doenitz,[19] and Jodl rushed up to him: "What did the Führer say?" They surrounded him, and Goebbels told them that Hitler considered the situation hopeless, he saw no more possibilities and thought the war was lost. He had broken down completely, never before had he seen him in such a state. Goebbels related, further, how shocked he had been when Hitler had told him, over the telephone, in a breaking voice, that he and his wife and children should move immediately into the Führerbunker, since this was the end.

Bormann was so agitated he could not stand still. He spoke alternately to Goebbels, Doenitz, Keitel, and again Doenitz, and repeated emphatically that Hitler must be persuaded by whatever means to leave Berlin. Goebbels asked Keitel in an undertone:

"Field Marshal, do you really see no possibility of arresting the Russian attack?"

It was in fact impossible to arrest the Russians. They had come to Berlin in order to smash the Third Reich completely. I asked Vasili Ivanovich Kazakov, Marshal of Artillery, about those Russian artillerymen whose fire on August 21 and 22 had so impressed Hitler. Kazakov, who was in command of the artillery units of the 1st Byelorussian Front in April 1945, confirmed that it had been the long-range guns of the Artillery Corps under General Likhachev. This corps had come from Leningrad to reinforce the artillery units of the 1st Byelorussian Front. Cities, as may be seen, can also revenge themselves.

[19] Here, and in what follows, Vice-Admiral Voss is mistaken for Doenitz.

1 3

5

There are other advantages which the historian can put to use: We now have access to a great number of authentic testimonies which give us insight into the thought processes and the political psychology of War Criminal Number One. Among them are the completely reliable records of the Military Conferences, as well as the revealing if somewhat less reliable—because recorded by Bormann—transcriptions of the "Table Talks," and the notes of Interpreter Paul Schmidt. This list I will now complement with a hitherto unknown document. It is the stenographic record from the series of Military Conferences, dated October 27, 1943, which carries the startling subtitle: "How can the war be ended victoriously?"

Did Hitler really have the formula for which he would no doubt today be offered half of the realm of those who are likewise unable to end victoriously a war in which they have become entrapped? What was Hitler's method?

"The crucial thing is to continue fighting ruthlessly and to damage the enemy as much as one can damage him, without ever losing heart, constantly on the alert for each weakness and exploiting it immediately, never allowing the slightest thought of capitulation or of a so-called agreement without some advantage. . . ."

Or:

"As long as one lies in wait like a cat and takes advantage of every moment to deal a sudden blow, one is not lost, possibilities will always arise. The other party will show elements of weakness. One must only stand ready to exploit them. . . ."

That, then, was the recipe with the help of which Hitler intended to win the war. There was another one. The Führer said:

"Who can be sure that one day a bomb won't explode among the Allies, that suddenly the existing tensions will not tear apart the plaster now covering them over."

Or:

"A single inner breakdown among the enemy could make the entire opposing front collapse."

The proof of the pudding is in the eating, and April 1945 revealed the true worth of the wisdom of Germany's Supreme War Lord.

In the spring of 1945, Adolf Hitler, Wilhelm Keitel, and Heinz Guderian had to realize that they were waiting in vain for elements of weakness in the Russian Army. From the cat, the German Armed Forces had been transformed into the mouse caught in the trap.

But might the other recipe have helped them to victory?

I do not make the claim that I can present my readers with every last detail of how intensively and by what channels an understanding between Hitler Germany and the Anglo-Saxon Western Powers was attempted. A great many publications deal with this subject, among them the memoirs of Himmler's Chief of Intelligence, Walter Schellenberg, and of his personal physician, Dr. Felix Kersten. Ample and varied material, both factual and analytical, is to be found in the works of Gerhard Ritter, Andreas Hillgruber, Hans Rothfels, Heinz Höhne, and others. The obvious conclusion is that the idea of an anti-Soviet plot matured in widely different circles.

It was forcefully advanced by the representatives of the military opposition, particularly by that wing which entertained direct contacts with American and English personalities. The idea of the plot was just as strongly advocated by a number of highly placed SS leaders, and quite particularly by the Chief of Office VI in the Reich Security Police, SS-General Walter Schellenberg, who, however, did not act on his own but in connivance with Reich Führer SS, Heinrich Himmler. The Foreign Minister, Joachim von Ribbentrop, who in earlier years had played the role of furtherer of British-German co-operation, also had views along these lines.

All these personalities were motivated in widely different ways, but on one point they concurred: they would try to split the united anti-Hitler front by the means of anti-Communism.

So far as I know, Hitler's own attitude to these projects has not yet been made the subject of a separate study. But it is possible to ascertain that Hitler was in no way disinclined to negotiate with the Western Allies. Especially toward the end of the war Hitler became intoxicated with the idea of dividing the combined front of his opponents. The testimonies of his former adjutant Otto Günsche typify his attitude.

In his notes Günsche mentions a remark of Hitler's made in November 1937 after his conversation with British Foreign Secretary Halifax. As Günsche remembers it, Hitler was delighted with the meeting on the Obersalzberg. Hitler commented afterwards, with great self-satisfaction:

"I have always said that the English will get under the same eiderdown with me; in their politics they follow the same guidelines as I do, namely, the overriding necessity to annihilate Bolshevism."

Toward the end of the war, in 1944, Hitler toyed with the thought of reviving this mutual interest. In the Soviet protocol of Günsche's interrogation we read:

> Whenever Hitler spoke of the increasing tensions in relations between the Western Powers and Soviet Russia, he stressed that now it was a case of playing for time. At that period, in September 1944, Hitler was convinced that the Anglo-Americans would be willing to make a separate peace with Germany, but would first request his resignation. This demand for Hitler's resignation was indeed made by the English during negotiations with representatives of the German Foreign Office in Stockholm. . . . As soon as Hitler heard of the English prerequisite, he broke off negotiations.

Ribbentrop's liaison official, Ambassador Hewel, vented his dissatisfaction after the breaking-off of the Stockholm negotiations in a conversation with Günsche. The war in the East, he said, had entered a stage which made peace with the Western Powers imperative.

16

"What is the Führer waiting for? He has to make a decision, to find a way out," was Hewel's comment.

Hitler's idea of a way out was a collision between the Western Powers and the Soviet Union. After his Military Conferences he used to say as a finishing touch: "Gentlemen, you will see that I will be proved right!"

According to Günsche, Hitler planned the Battle of the Bulge at the end of 1944 in order to maneuver the Western Powers into a separate peace. During the offensive in January 1945, Hitler announced to his adjutants:

"I will show these Englishmen that peace with Germany can be made only with me and not without me!"

Once the offensive had broken down and the Supreme Command of the German Armed Forces had to transfer the 6th SS Panzer Army to the Eastern front, Hitler openly declared that the plan for a separate peace with the Western Allies had miscarried.

But the idea was by no means dropped. Here we may recall, as one instance among others, Himmler's offer to Eisenhower, stating that "the SS and the Armed Forces would be willing to continue the war against Russia if the Anglo-Americans would enter into an armistice with us. . . . I agree to acknowledge the victory of the Western Powers. Should they leave me the weapons, I will still be able to do this." [1]

Even the contacts with SS-Obergruppenführer Karl Wolff, former Chief of Himmler's personal staff, established toward the end of the war with Allen Dulles in Italy, were obviously planned with Hitler's approval. In Martin Bormann's diary, a copy of which I possess, it is noted that SS-Obergruppenführer Wolff was received by Hitler on February 6, 1945.

Günsche also testified that, in conversation with Albert Speer during the final weeks, Hitler had repeatedly stressed that it would be necessary to re-establish the old ties between German industrialists and their British and American counterparts. Hitler commented:

[1] Felix Kersten, *Memoirs 1940-1945* (London, 1956).

"The development on the Eastern front will lead inescapably to a military understanding between Germany, England, and America directed against the Bolshevik threat; in this connection, the industrialists will have to play a foremost role."

I consider this testimony of Günsche's all the more pertinent since I have in my possession the copy of a message which Albert Speer sent to Secretary of State Karl-Hermann Frank in Prague on April 23, 1945:

I proposed to the Führer today that Czech industrialists should fly to France. The Führer gave his approval. Plane held ready. Bearer of this message will give detailed instructions concerning the plane. I hope that this action initiated by you will prove successful. Enclosed memo from Reich Minister for Foreign Affairs for your information.

P.S. Please destroy papers after reading.

What kind of mission the Czech industrialists would have been charged with can be seen from Ribbentrop's enclosed letter. Only a carbon copy without signature is extant, but from internal evidence it is the document mentioned by Speer:

At the suggestion of Reich Minister Speer I proposed to the Führer that Czech industrialists be permitted to fly to France in order to begin negotiations with their American contacts there with the aim of protecting Czechoslovakia from the Bolsheviks.

Günsche reports further:

Hitler accused Ribbentrop of not having pushed sufficiently his plan for a separate peace with England and America. On the same day, Bormann said to Hitler:

"My Führer, it is high time for you yourself to make contact with the Americans."

Hitler answered in a resigned tone of voice:

"I no longer have sufficient authority for that. Somebody else must do this."

Certain people may consider these attempts of the leadership of the Third Reich to establish a political and military alliance with the United States and England as remarkable political farsightedness on the part of Hitler, Himmler, and Ribbentrop. Did they not plan as far back as 1945 what Adenauer and Dulles consummated in 1949 and 1954? However, kinship with Hitler's political mentality can hardly be thought a badge of honor, least of all for the creators of NATO. In reading Himmler's memoranda addressed to Montgomery and Eisenhower, or the protocols of the secret talks between German and American emissaries, their resemblance to the propaganda of the Atlantic Pact becomes striking. In all these documents the same formulas recur: again there is the necessity to ward off the "Communist threat," the call to come to a reckoning with the Soviet Union.

Another hitherto unpublished detail is found in Günsche's records: During a conference in January or February 1945, Martin Bormann gave the order for a group of his people to go underground in West Germany, with the injunction, however, to behave loyally toward the American occupation authorities, so as to prepare the future rebirth of the National Socialist Party.

One of the participants in the conference noted the following remark made by Bormann: "Our salvation lies in the West. Only there will we be able to keep our Party alive. The slogan 'Fight Communism' will be its guarantee of survival. . . ." In the postwar years these same words have been as glibly used by some West German adherents of NATO.

Even when Soviet soldiers had penetrated the outskirts of Berlin, Hitler still clung to his belief: "If I defeat the enemy here and hold the capital, the English and the Americans may perhaps conceive the hope that eventually they can confront this danger together with Nazi Germany. . . . In this case the

19

enemy may still come to believe that there is only one person able to stop the Bolshevik colossus, and that is me, together with the Party and the present German State." Goebbels, the Minister of Propaganda, encouraged this hope: "Our opponents themselves concede that the enemy coalition is ripe for a split. They are speaking of a Third World War, etc. The concept of a Third World War is an established term in the Anglo-American Press." [1]

Hitler, Goebbels, and Ribbentrop lived in a world of illusions. This was not yet the year 1954. In 1945 the reaction of the Western Powers toward plans for an anti-Soviet understanding with Germany was understandably different from that in the Adenauer period. The war was still on, the watershed between the wrestling coalitions was clearly defined, and the world was aware that the real enemy was Hitler. Also, the United States would have had no use for such a bankrupt ally.

6

But illusions also have their practical sides. No matter how chimerical the hopes that Roosevelt and Churchill might turn their arms against the Soviet Army five minutes before the victorious end, these hopes served the Nazi leaders as excuse to continue a senseless and criminal war which at this stage had turned into a war against the German people.

The illusions of the bunker proved most disastrous for those hundreds of thousands of German soldiers and officers on the Eastern front who, obeying catastrophic orders, had to hold their fronts to the finish. Upheld by the chimera of an alliance with the West, Hitler, the High Command of the Armed Forces, and the General Staff performed the psychological and demagogical trick of spurring their soldiers on to endure and persist in hopeless positions.

[1] Quotations from Military Conferences dated April 25, 1945, published for the first time in *Der Spiegel*, No. 3, 1966.

A special role was assigned to Field Marshal Ferdinand Schörner, who was instructed to retreat with his Army Group to the so-called National Redoubt,[1] and to continue resistance from there. Hitler summoned Schörner several times to the Chancellery in order to give him personal instructions. Schörner was known for total submission to his War Lord's orders and for the brutality with which he carried them out. Not for nothing did Hitler name him in his Political Testament as his successor as Chief of the Armed Forces.

While the Twilight of the Gods was enacted in the Chancellery, German soldiers continued to fight and die in a lost cause for "Führer, Nation, and Country"—not just in and around Berlin, but also in Kurland, on the Frische Nehrung, at the Weichsel estuary, and on the Hela Peninsula. They continued to fight and die even after Hitler's death, for Grand Admiral Karl Doenitz, his successor, together with Keitel and Jodl, persevered in Hitler's course after having taken over the office of President of the Reich and Supreme Commander.

As late as early May, a special courier of the General Staff, Lieutenant Colonel Ulrich de Maizière, had been dispatched to the Army High Command, East Prussia, to keep the Army from ceasing fire. Unable to find air transportation, Maizière could not reach the Army Staff in person and therefore had to transmit the last order in written form. It is owing to this accident that we know the precise contents of the order. After his return to the "seat of Government" in Flensburg, the courier of the General Staff submitted a report, which, together with all other documents of the Doenitz government, was later seized by the Allies.

Here is the text of the report:

Since to report in person in Hela would have involved a delay of two to three days for me, an officer of the High Command of Army Group Kurland is delivering the oral

---

[1] This, supposed to be a last stronghold of Nazi resistance in the alpine regions of southern Bavaria and Austria, never materialized.

21

instructions for Army East Prussia. They are summarized in the following:

1. Data for the personal information of the High Command and Chief. Passing on strictly prohibited.
2. The Führer has appointed Grand Admiral Doenitz as new President of the Reich, government seat at present Flensburg, Prague area to be considered as a last resort. Advisers to the Grand Admiral, Foreign Minister Count Schwerin Krosigk, Reichsführer SS in his capacity of Minister of the Interior, Minister of the Reich Speer, Secretary of State Heiler [2] for the Ministry of Food.
3. Should Grand Admiral transfer to Prague, High Command North to go to Field Marshal Busch with Staff Kinzel,[3] with command over Army East Prussia.
4. Chief mission of Grand Admiral: The rescue of as many Germans and as much German territory as possible from Bolshevism. Therefore continuance of fighting against Russia. Negotiations in progress with Western Powers. These already initiated
   a) by a delegation OKW (Admiral von Friedeburg as new Commander-in-Chief of the Navy, General Kinzel, Admiral [4] Wagner) with Montgomery;
   b) by Field Marshal Kesselring with the Americans;
   c) by General (Generaloberst) v. Vietinghoff (Southwest) with Marshal Alexander. Outcome still pending.
5. Commentary to the Instruction transmitted on May 5 by Fu Fe (WFST.g.Kdos. Restricted to Chief).
   Aim: Evacuation of as many people as possible from the Army sector into the Western territory of the Reich. Number restricted because of lack of fuel oil and coal. Possible number for Army not yet fully established, provisionally ca. 60-70,000. Negotiations in progress with Western Powers concerning tacit toleration of evacuation, possibly

[2] Probably Secretary of State Dr. Hayler, from the Ministry of Economy.
[3] Chief of Staff North.
[4] Should be Rear Admiral.

22

*Dr. Faust Shkaravski,
head of Autopsy Commission*

*Lieutenant General
Ivan Klimenko,
head of search party*

Hitler's burning (x) *and burying* (xx) *site in front of bunker exit* (xxx)

even furtherance of same. Outcome pending. Subordinate posts to be informed only of substance and motivation of order.

6. Selection of persons to be evacuated by Army:
Besides the wounded, women and children, only valuable persons, no prisoners, foreigners, etc. Only light weapons to be taken along. Everything else to be destroyed. Only horses and horse-drawn vehicles to be offered to peasant population.

7. For those remaining behind, fighting power Hela to be strengthened as much as possible, in anticipation of further evacuation; provisioning from Reich territory possible only in restricted measure.

8. Grand Admiral and Chief WFST fully aware of gravity of decision and its possible repercussion on Army, but no other possibility open to escape seizure by Russians; making every effort to obtain toleration of evacuation and increase of tonnage by way of negotiations. This message specially important to Chief WFST.

9. Sincerely regret that air transportation from here to Hela no longer available and therefore personal report to High Command and Herr General possible only with great delay, permission for which I was not granted.[5]

Thus far the text of the order which the liaison officer for the Army Staff delivered to the Army Staff in the pocket on the Weichsel estuary. Was this order dictated by concern for the soldiers of Army Group "East Prussia"? I doubt it, for in substance the order amounted to a death sentence. It was handed over on May 4, that is, after the fall of Berlin, and a few days before the revolt in Prague. Farcical indeed was the sentence about the "rescue of as many Germans as possible from Bolshevism." This order actually led to the death of as

[5] This document is dated 4.4.1945, but this is an obvious mistake. At the bottom the document carries a handwritten addendum stating that it was submitted May 4.

many Germans as possible. Or did Doenitz and his generals wish to anticipate the familiar slogan of the Cold War: Rather dead than red?

This case proves abundantly that the lie about "negotiations" with the Western Allies was used in order to maintain soldiers and officers in their senseless resistance. Could one seriously count on the Western Allies for help in the evacuation of German troops from the Eastern front? I asked Admiral Nikolai Kuznetsov, who at the time was in command of the Soviet Navy, whether any English or American battleships were operating in the Baltic.

"Absolutely none," Kuznetsov answered. "In the Baltic, units of our Navy only were operating, covering the advance of our land troops. Of course we also attacked enemy shipping trying to evacuate troops from Kurland and East Prussia. I very much doubt that the English Navy could have intervened there; its ships were operating many hundreds of miles away, behind Öresund and the Belt."

"And their air force?"

"The Allied air force did operate in this area; the English, for instance, frequently bombed Danzig. But it would be an absurdity to say that the English air force might have tried to give 'cover,' on May 4, 1945, to the evacuation of German troops from the Hela Peninsula."

Ever since the days of the Doenitz government, the argument has been reiterated that the delaying action of the Germans in Kurland and East Prussia saved thousands of German soldiers from Russian captivity, by making it possible for them to reach the West in time and become prisoners of the English. I find this argument highly specious, for three reasons: First, thousands of German soldiers and officers had to pay with their lives for the escape of a few ships from East Prussia to the future British Occupation Zone. Marshal Alexander Mikhailovich Vasilevski, at the time Commander-in-Chief of the 3rd Byelorussian Front, confirmed that the German troops at the Vistula estuary and on the Frische Nehrung did indeed offer

24

fierce resistance which naturally provoked a corresponding reaction on the Soviet side.

Finally, and quite particularly in the case of East Prussia, one should keep in mind that Hitler himself had brought about the catastrophe that engulfed many thousands of soldiers and civilians there. His adjutant Günsche furnished eloquent proof for this:

When the German troops had been forced to retreat, Hitler ordered his army adjutant (Major Willy Johannmeyer) to fly to the East Prussian front, study the situation there, and report to him. Hitler was anxious to check on the reports of the German Army commanders in East Prussia, partly because, as usual, he did not want to give credence to unpleasant news, and partly because he believed that everything was put in a false light in order to avoid heavy fighting against the Russians.

On his return, Johannmeyer confirmed the grave situation of the German troops in East Prussia. He reported that the troops were huddled together on a small coastal strip, interspersed with thousands of refugees and herds of cattle; for this reason each shell from the Russian artillery caused severe losses.

Hitler countered: "I will not withdraw a single soldier from our lines. I have to hold on to the fortress of Königsberg no matter what the cost. As long as we hold Königsberg, I may truthfully tell the German people: 'It's we who hold East Prussia, not the Russians.'"

When Johannmeyer reported on the chaotic mass flight of the East Prussian people, adding that this would mean annihilation for a great many among them, Hitler shouted: "I can't take that into consideration."

Even if one takes such pronouncements as the ravings of his ruthless fury needing to vent itself in an outburst against the German people, this mentality is by no means typical for only

2 5

the last year of the war. As early as November 27, 1941—
ironically at the very time when the German troops bogged
down before Moscow—Hitler told the Danish Minister of Foreign Affairs, Skavenius:

"Should the German people ever fail to be sufficiently strong
and self-sacrificing to risk its blood for its existence, it might
just as well disappear and be annihilated by another, stronger
power. It would have lost its right to the place that it has
conquered at this moment." [6]

And Goebbels, in his valedictory speech to his collaborators
at the Ministry of Propaganda, declared cynically:

"The German people, the German people, what can one do
with a people that refuses to go on fighting! All the plans and
goals of National Socialism were too noble to appeal to this
people. It was too cowardly to make them come true. It flees
from the East, in the West it hinders the soldiers from fighting
and welcomes the enemy with white flags. The German people
deserves the fate that it expects." [7]

Hitler at any rate wanted to continue the war beyond the
twelfth hour, just as he had previously vowed not to stop "five
minutes before twelve." More than once he threatened in front
of his accomplices to let the entire German people perish if
Germany should lose the war: "If the German people shows
no readiness to fight for its self-preservation, it had better
perish."

During the Nuremberg Trials, the entire world learned from
Albert Speer how Hitler reacted when he was faced with the
collapse of his Reich: "If the war is lost, the people will also
be lost. This fate is incontrovertible. . . . The nation will have
proved itself the weaker one. . . . Those who remain after the
battle will in any case only be the inferior ones."

The atrocities committed against other peoples now acted
as a boomerang. On September 7, 1943, Himmler had ordered
SS-Obergruppenführer Prützmann "to leave behind in the

---

[6] *Staatsmänner und Diplomaten bei Hitler* (Frankfurt/Main 1967).
[7] Jürgen Thorwald, *Das Ende an der Elbe* (Stuttgart, 1959), pp. 59-60.

Ukraine not a single person, no cattle, not a ton of grain, not a railroad track." Now the same Prützmann, in his capacity as Commander of "Werewolf," was ordered to execute special tasks in the rear of the enemy—he was to destroy buildings, bridges, and the like. However, the territory in the enemy's rear was no longer the Ukraine, but Germany.

There can be no doubt: the "Führer" aimed to destroy the bases of the German people's existence. And he intended to take along with him to the grave as many of his compatriots as possible.

7

While Soviet Counter Intelligence officers searched the garden of the Chancellery on May 2 in ignorance of what they might find there, the highest Soviet Command Posts had already received a number of testimonies regarding Hitler's death. The official German evidence came with a letter that Goebbels and Bormann had sent to Stalin.

I myself have held this letter in my hand. I was summoned early in the morning of May 1 to Marshal Georgi Konstantinovich Zhukov. The staff of his Army was stationed in Strausberg, a suburb of Berlin. We officers of the staff were billeted in private houses, but for reasons of safety Staff Headquarters had ordered the excavation of deep, comfortable bunkers, in which the Command Post was housed. When I descended into the bunker and reported my presence, the Chief of Staff of the 1st Byelorussian Front, Senior General Mikhail Sergeyevich Malinin, handed me several sheets of paper on which I noticed unusually large letters. We learned later that this was the type face of the famous "Führer typewriter." Hitler's eyes were weak, but he refused to wear glasses, so all documents had to be in large letters. The letter to Stalin which informed him that Hitler had departed this world had been typed with this same Führer type.

I translated immediately from the German into Russian. Marshal Zhukov, who was sitting next to a large map, listened attentively and asked an occasional question whenever something appeared doubtful to him—for instance, after the sentence in which the authors of the letter wrote that they informed Stalin of Hitler's death as "first among non-Germans." The contents of the letter were relayed sentence by sentence over the telephone to Moscow, where a general of the STAVKA was on duty at that end of the line. I learned later that the Supreme Chief of the Armed Forces, Stalin, was immediately informed.

The officers of the Army Staff who had been with Chuikov told me that the letter had been delivered personally at night by the Acting Chief of the German General Staff, General Krebs, to the Commander in Chief of the 8th Guards Army, Vasili Chuikov, who was asked to transmit it. From his verbal commentaries in his conversation with Chuikov and with the deputy of Marshal Zhukov, General of the Army Vasili Danilovich Sokolovski, it could be deduced that Hitler had committed suicide.

I cannot say that those who read the Goebbels-Bormann letter at dawn on May 1, 1945, fully believed in the events it described. I therefore doubt whether the news contained in this letter was forwarded to the 3rd Assault Detachment whose officers at the time had the order to search the area of the Chancellery. The documents delivered by Krebs were immediately passed on from the Staff of the 8th Guards Army to the Army Supreme Command, and from there they were transmitted to Moscow. They bore the stamp "Secret." At any rate no one would have announced the contents of a letter to troops in the midst of battle.

On May 2 the previously mentioned Otto Günsche was taken prisoner, and his copious testimony regarding the Führer's death became available. He had, however, been caught on the outskirts of the city (outside of the fighting sector of the 3rd Assault Detachment) and his testimony became known only much later. Some people had been taken prisoner in the immediate vicinity of the Chancellery, but their testimony about Hitler's death was very vague. A man called Mengershausen, who had been an eyewitness to the burning, was made prisoner by Soviet troops somewhat later.

The Soviet Intelligence officers did not have much time for deliberations: they had orders to start the search immediately. The action was directed by Lieutenant Colonel Ivan Isayevich Klimenko, Commander of the Counter Intelligence Section, 79th Rifle Corps. Klimenko, a professional soldier since 1936, had started on his way to Berlin in the memorable year 1941 at Yelnya, where he had his first encounter with the Germans. Five times he was caught in encircling battles, and in extricating himself he had marched, on foot, approximately 1100 km. He arrived at the Chancellery, however, in an Army truck. With him in the truck were three other officers, and in a truck following them there were five soldiers.

They owed their mission to the fortuitous accident that the Chancellery had become part of the fighting sector of their Corps. This 79th Rifle Corps under the command of Major General Pepevertkin had advanced in the battle from the north toward the Reichstag Building and the Chancellery. The 150th Division under Brigadier General Zhatilov had hoisted the red banner on the German Parliament, a building which Zhukov had pointed out to his Armies as a widely visible goal. Simultaneously, the 301st Division under General Antonov, which belonged to the 5th Shock Army of General Berzarin and was advancing from the south, had occupied the Gestapo Building in Prinz Albrecht Strasse and the adjacent Air Ministry Building. At dawn on May 1 the gunners of the 301st Division posted their cannons in front of the Chancellery.

Shortly after noon new parliamentaries sent by Chancellor Goebbels appeared in the forward positions. General Antonov refused to negotiate: fighting soon broke out again, but it did not last long, for in the dusk another group of officers appeared with a white flag. This time they announced Goebbels' suicide. The final capitulation of the remnants of the Berlin garrison came on the morning of the following day, May 2, 1945, under orders of their commander, General Weidling.

In the afternoon of that day Lieutenant Colonel Klimenko of the 3rd Shock Army received orders to inspect the building which soldiers of the 5th Shock Army had stormed the night before: the Chancellery.

It was a somewhat unusual task. No existing instructions of Soviet Intelligence told how to deal with the nucleus of the Fascist Reich. But it is not the habit of the Soviet Army to wait inactively for instructions. The Counter Intelligence officers, the search personnel of the 79th Corps, and the entire 3rd Shock Army had prepared ahead of the attack on Berlin (no one doubting of its success) for this special task: the seizure of important documents, capture of the main war criminals, destruction of the enemy Intelligence net, etc. Now it is Klimenko's turn to speak:

After the 79th Rifle Corps had occupied the Parliament building, my detachment was billeted in Plötzensee Prison; members of the German Armed Forces made prisoners in the area of the Parliament and the Chancellery were taken there. Naturally, we questioned them about the fate of the leaders of the Fascist Reich, above all about Hitler and Goebbels. Several among them said that they had heard of Hitler's and Goebbels' suicide in the Chancellery. On May 2 I therefore decided to take along four witnesses and to drive with them to the Chancellery.

It was afternoon and it rained. I climbed into a jeep, the witnesses and soldiers into an Army truck. We drove up to the Chancellery, went into the garden, and arrived at the emergency exit of the Führerbunker. As we approached this exit, one of the Germans shouted: "That is Goebbels' corpse! That is the corpse of his wife!"

I decided to take these corpses with us. Since we did not have a stretcher, we placed the corpses on an unhinged door,

3 0

maneuvered them onto the truck (it was a covered vehicle), and returned to Plötzensee.

The day after, May 3, 1945, the corpses of six Goebbels children and the corpse of General Krebs were found in the bunker. They too were taken to Plötzensee.

Later some generals and officers from the staffs of the 3rd Shock Army and the 1st Byelorussian Front came over, and also the Soviet war correspondents Martin Merzhanov and Boris Garbatov. Now the procedure of identification began.

This was done in the following manner: Goebbels' body was laid in a room on the table, the bodies of his wife and children and that of General Krebs were put on the floor. The witnesses were kept in another room. The first to enter the room was Vice-Admiral Voss, the representative of Grand Admiral Doenitz at Führer headquarters; he had been captured by members of the Counter Intelligence Section of the 3rd Shock Army. Without hesitating he identified Goebbels and his children. The other witnesses did the same.

Goebbels' death was proved beyond any doubt. The care taken by the Soviet Counter Intelligence officers should be lauded: in order to exclude the slightest chance of error, they had the body of the Minister identified by nearly twenty witnesses.[1]

Now we let Klimenko speak again:

Naturally we asked Voss where Hitler might be. Voss gave no clear answer and told us only that he had left Berlin together with Hitler's adjutant, who had told him that Hitler had committed suicide and that his corpse had been burned in the Chancellery garden.

After the questioning I decided to go back to the Chancellery and try to find some clues there.

[1] The examination continued even after the signing of the protocol. When the chief of Goebbels' bodyguard, Wilhelm Echold, had been captured, he too was confronted with the body, and he also confirmed the identity.

We arrived with the jeep carrying me, Voss, a Lieutenant Colonel of the Army Counter Intelligence Service, and an interpreter. At the Chancellery, we went down into the bunker. It was dark. We illuminated our way with flashlights. Voss behaved somewhat strangely; he was nervous, mumbling unintelligibly. After that we climbed up again and found ourselves in the garden, not far from the emergency exit.

It was close to 9 P.M. We stepped up to a big dried-up water tank for fire-fighting. It was filled with many corpses. Here Voss said, pointing to a corpse: "Oh, this is Hitler's body!"

This corpse was dressed, the feet were in mended socks. After a moment Voss began to have his doubts: "No, no, I can't say with certainty that it is Hitler." Frankly, I also had my doubts because of the mended socks!

At this hour I was somewhat in a hurry, and the Lieutenant Colonel of Counter Intelligence, who was in charge of Voss, even more so. We resolved to drive back, but once in Plötzensee I asked my collaborators to search among the prisoners for anyone who had known Hitler personally and might assist in the identification.

Then came May 4. From early morning the search among the prisoners for possible witnesses went on. Around 11 A.M. I returned to the garden of the Chancellery together with six witnesses. We ran to the water tank, but the corpse had already vanished!

I wanted to enter the building but was not admitted, for by this time the Chancellery was part of the sector of the 5th Shock Army. I had first to get myself an entry permit from the Command Post, which was in another wing of the Chancellery. The corpse we had found the day before was laid out in one of the many halls. Only one of the six witnesses said it might be Hitler. The other five denied it categorically.

I learned from officers there that they were waiting for a

Soviet diplomat who might help in the identification. That was approximately around noon.

Together with me were Platoon Leader Panassov and a few soldiers. One of my soldiers asked: "Where did you find Goebbels?" We went back to the garden, to the bunker exit.

Private Ivan Churakov climbed into a nearby crater that was strewn with burned paper. I noticed a bazooka in there and called to Churakov: "Climb out quickly, or you may be blown to bits!" Churakov answered: "Comrade Lieutenant Colonel, there are legs here!"

We started to dig them out and pulled two corpses from the crater: the bodies of a man and a woman. Of course at first I didn't even think that these might be the corpses of Hitler and Eva Braun, since I believed that Hitler's corpse was already in the Chancellery and only needed to be identified. I therefore ordered the corpses to be wrapped in blankets and reburied. Inside the Chancellery identification proceedings continued. . . .

No one among the officers and generals of the 1st Byelorussian Front had ever set eyes on Hitler. But in expectation of the signing of the surrender, Soviet diplomats arrived in Berlin whose testimony might have considerable weight. Klimenko remembers that a group of generals surrounding a man in diplomat's uniform appeared about 2 P.M. in the Chancellery. The diplomat immediately ascertained that this was not Hitler's body: "You can safely bury him again. . . ."

This prompted Klimenko to reconsider Ivan Churakov's find. Early in the morning of May 5 he returned with Churakov's replacement Deryabin and the driver Tsybochkin to the garden in order to dig the crater up again. The two corpses were pulled out. For this reason the protocol quoted earlier on the discovery of the corpses is dated not the 4th but the 5th of May. In this ditch they now also found the corpses of two dogs. Another protocol was made about this find.

Where is the man who found Hitler's body, where is Ivan

Churakov now? I was unable to trace him and unable, therefore, to chart the life of the man who played such a decisive role in those days. He was one of the millions of simple soldiers who carried the tremendous load of the Great Patriotic War.

Millions of people in the Soviet Union are, like him, called Ivan. Hundreds of thousands of Soviet soldiers and officers bear the same humble Russian name which seems to stand for something specifically Russian. In the Third Reich, it was often used disparagingly; in countless pieces of SS propaganda, the Russians were sneered at as "Ivans," subhuman beings, who could only serve as slaves to the German overlords.

As the war went on, the word changed meaning: in the last days of the war it was pronounced with respect, even with fear. "Ivan," the supposedly subhuman being, had shown himself a giant capable of surmounting all the obstacles of the war. Ivan came to Berlin and found the corpse of War Criminal Number One.

8

Today we are able to indicate with topographical precision the exact spot where Hitler was burned and buried. Klimenko and his group returned within a week to the garden of the Chancellery, after the bodies had been identified and the forensic autopsies had been concluded. But the professional sense of an Intelligence officer accustomed to checking his findings again and again brought Klimenko back to the "scene of the crime."

Soviet patrols had in the meantime uncovered an SS man who turned out to have been one of the Führer's bodyguards. He was Harry Mengershausen (in Klimenko's documents he is spelled by mistake Mengeshausen). In his capacity as eyewitness he was asked to indicate precisely how and where Hitler's corpse had been burned and buried. Once he had overcome his fear, he led the Soviet officers to the same crater in which Ivan Churakov had discovered the bodies. The following testimony was drawn up:

RECORD
Re   *Burying site of the bodies of Adolf Hitler and his wife*

1945, the 13th day May
Berlin

We, the undersigned: Chief, Counter Intelligence Section SMERSH, 79th Rifle Corps, Lieutenant Colonel Klimenko; Chief Examining Magistrate, Counter Intelligence Section SMERSH, Katyshev; Chief, Ordnance-Surveyor Squad, 79th Rifle Corps, Major of the Guards Gabelok; Second Lieutenant Kalashnikov; Privates, Special Platoon, Counter Intelligence Section SMERSH, 79th Rifle Corps, Oleynik, Churakov, Navash, Myalkin, accompanied by the witness Mengeshausen, Harry, investigated on this day the spot where the corpses of the German Chancellor of the Reich Adolf Hitler and his wife were buried.

Witness Mengeshausen, Harry, attested that he, as member of the SS Combat Group Mundtkes,[1] had been detailed from April 20 to 30 to the defense of the Chancellery area and the personal protection of Adolf Hitler.

On April 30, 1945, around noon, he was on guard within the building of the New Chancellery, where it was his duty to cover the hallway passing Hitler's study and continuing to the blue dining room.[2]

On his tour of duty through the above-mentioned hallway Mengeshausen stopped in the blue dining room in front of the farthest window, which is closest to the exit to the garden, and observed what went on in the Chancellery garden.

At this moment Sturmbannführer Günsche and Linge carried the bodies of Adolf Hitler and his wife Ifa Braun[3] (his

[1] Thus in the Russian text. Chief of the Combat Group in charge of the defense of the Government sector was SS-Brigadeführer and Major General of the Waffen SS, Wilhelm Mohnke.
[2] The designation "blue dining room" frequently recurs in Klimenko's documents; it must be the so-called Hall of Mosaics.
[3] Thus in the Russian text.

35

private secretary [4]) from the emergency exit into the open. This roused his interest and he watched carefully to see how things developed.

Hitler's personal adjutant Günsche poured gasoline over the bodies and ignited them. After half an hour the bodies of Hitler and his wife were consumed; they were taken to a crater at about one meter's distance from the above-mentioned emergency exit, and there buried.

The entire procedure—the carrying out of the corpses, their cremation, and the burial of the bodies of Adolf Hitler and his wife—was personally observed by Mengeshausen from a distance of 600 meters.[5]

Mengeshausen further attested that, on April 29, Hitler's dog also was buried in the crater. Distinguishing features: a tall shepherd with long ears, black back, and light flanks. From Paul Phenie,[6] who was in special charge of the dog, Mengeshausen learned that he had been poisoned.

On investigating the places Mengeshausen had indicated, his deposition was found to be correct. During his tour of duty on April 30, 1945, Mengeshausen could observe quite clearly from the window of the blue dining room what went on near the emergency exit of the Führerbunker. The testimony of the witness Mengeshausen is all the more credible since we pulled from the designated crater on " " May 1945 [7] the corpses of a man and a woman disfigured by fire and two poisoned dogs which, as was recognized by other witnesses, belonged to Hitler and his private secretary Ifa Braun.

A diagram of the place where the corpses of Hitler and his wife were discovered, as well as photographs of the place indicated by witness Mengeshausen, is appended.

Deposition drawn up in the Chancellery, city of Berlin.

[4] She was never Hitler's secretary.
[5] Thus in the Russian text (actually the distance is only 60 meters).
[6] Name unidentifiable.
[7] Date left open in text.

Chief, Counter Intelligence Section SMERSH
79th Rifle Corps
Lieutenant Colonel
signed   (Klimenko)

Chief Examining Magistrate and Interpreter,
Counter Intelligence Section SMERSH, 79th RC
Senior Lieutenant
signed   (Katyshev)

Chief, Ordnance-Surveyor Squad, 79th RC
Major of the Guards
signed   (Gabelok)

Photographer-Correspondent, 79th RC
Second Lieutenant
signed   (Kalashnikov)

Privates, Counter Intelligence Section
SMERSH, 79th RC
signed   (Olcynik)
          (Churakov)
          (Navash)
          (Myalkin)

Witness
signed   (Mengeshausen)

There are two important addenda to the record, a diagram of
the place of discovery with explanatory text by the topographer.
(See Illustrations.)

This ends the part of our story which took place in the garden
of the Chancellery. On orders of Marshal Zhukov, this former
combat territory had been placed under the command of the
5th Shock Army. The Staff of the 3rd Shock Army was transferred to the northern part of the town. Klimenko reports that
the bodies of Hitler, Eva Braun, and the two dogs were wrapped
in blankets, then put in wooden boxes, carried out of the Chan-

cellery early on May 5, and taken to the Counter Intelligence premises of the 3rd Shock Army.

9

On May 5, the scene shifted from the center of Berlin to the northern Berlin suburb of Buch, where various divisions of the Staff of the 3rd Shock Army were stationed. Klimenko's search platoon had fulfilled its task, but some questions were still open. *The first question* was whether the bodies that had been sought had really been found. *The second question* concerned the cause of their death. The first question had to be answered by Counter Intelligence personnel, criminologists, and physicians; the second was exclusively in the physicians' domain.

In place of the soldier Ivan a new character comes to the fore —Dr. Faust Shkaravski. I have not invented his first name: it is really the name of a man of advanced age, forensic physician by profession, who at the time was Chief Expert of Forensic Medicine with the 1st Byelorussian Front. Since then, Dr. Faust Yosifovich Shkaravski, Colonel in the Medical Service, has retired from active service. He permitted me to interview him in his Kiev apartment.

You, and not only you, are puzzled by my name. This is how I received it: My father was a modest employee in a sugar factory in Luchany, not far from Kiev, a simple soul with a hankering for culture and educated people. That is why he chose as my godparents the district physician and his daughter; they selected this name for me.

I myself am half Ukrainian, half Polish, but I consider myself a purely Soviet physician: in 1925 I graduated from the Medical Institute in Kiev. We were the first generation of Soviet physicians in the Ukraine. I became district physician and in 1929 entered the field of forensic medicine. Later I became county physician and was on the faculty of forensic medicine at the Kiev Medical Institute and the Institute for

Soldiers Deryabin and Tsybochkin during disinterment of the corpses of Hitler and Eva Braun

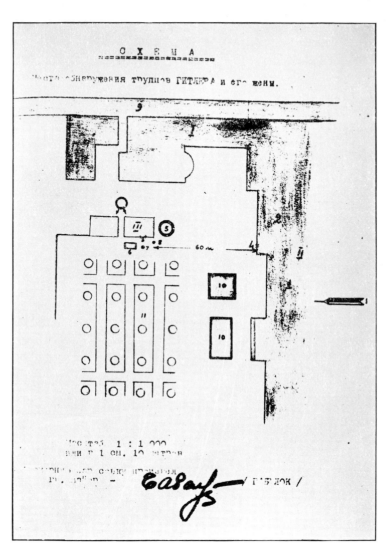

Diagram of site of Hitler's burial

УСЛОВНЫЕ ОБОЗНАЧЕНИЯ
================================

К схеме места обнаружения трупов
ГИТЛЕРА и его жены

1. Старая имперская канцелярия
II. Новая имперская канцелярия
III. Бункер ГИТЛЕРА

1. Рабочая комната ГИТЛЕРА
2. Голубая столовая
3. Запасной выход из бункера ГИТЛЕРА
4. Крайнее окно голубой столовой
5. Наблюдательная башня
6. Воронка
7. Место сожжения трупов ГЕББЕЛЬСА и его жены
8. Место сожжения ГИТЛЕРА и его жены
9. Вельгельм Штрассе
10. Водная бассейн
11. Парк

ГВАРДИИ МАЙОР -   / ГАБЕЛОК /

" 13 " мая 1945 года

Key to diagram

Key to the diagram of the site where the bodies of Hitler and his wife were found

I.	The old Chancellery	5.	Observation tower
II.	The new Chancellery	6.	Crater
III.	Hitler's bunker	7.	Site where the bodies of Goebbels and his wife were burned
1.	Hitler's study	8.	Site where Hitler and his wife were burned
2.	The blue dining room		
3.	Emergency exit from Hitler's bunker	9.	Wilhelm Strasse
4.	End window of the blue dining room	10.	Water tank
		11.	Park

Major of the Guards
May 13, 1945   / Gabelok /

Box with Hitler's corpse

Box with Eva Braun's corpse

Advanced Medical Studies. Shortly before the war broke out I was sent to the Leningrad Academy of Military Medicine. The war started and I returned to Kiev. I participated in the battles of Stalingrad and Kursk and advanced to Chief Expert of Forensic Medicine, first with the Don Front, later with the Central Front, and finally with the 1st Byelorussian Front. After the war I was formally awarded my medical doctorate.

As forensic medical expert I performed approximately a thousand autopsies. I was familiar with the methods and procedures, having instructed students in anatomy. At the beginning of May 1945, I was summoned by General Barabanov, Chief of Medical Services with the 1st Byelorussian Front. Barabanov told me that General Telegin, a member of the Military Council of the Byelorussian Front, had requested a forensic-medical expert opinion in a highly important matter. He signed my travel permit himself, and I drove immediately by car to Berlin-Buch to the 3rd Shock Army.

Konstantin Fedorovich Telegin—now Lieutenant General, ret., recalled clearly what happened:

"I did indeed issue such an order: I had been called from Moscow and ordered to get expert opinions on the corpses of the Fascist leaders that had been discovered and about which we had informed Moscow. The corpse of Goebbels had been found earlier, on May 2."

"Did this order also apply to Hitler's corpse?"

"At the time we did not know whether his corpse would be found. But the order applied to all that might be discovered. . . ."

On May 5 Dr. Faust Shkaravski entered a small house standing in a yard under guard. According to his report, there were nine corpses laid out in an unfurnished room.[1] Later he was joined in Buch by other medical experts: Krayevski, Marants, Gulkevich, Boguslavski.

When I appeared early in 1968 in the office of the corresponding member of the Academy of Medical Sciences of the

[1] The Goebbels family and General Krebs. The other corpses were brought later.

USSR, Professor Dr. Nikolai Alexandrovich Krayevski, he was most astonished by the subject of my inquiry. "Yes, I am the same Krayevski who together with Dr. Shkaravski signed the protocol. I did not think that I would have to come back to the subject again."

N. A. Krayevski, one of the foremost Soviet specialists in anatomical pathology, during the war was Chief Anatomical Pathologist with the 1st Byelorussian Front, and by the end of the war Chief Anatomical Pathologist of the entire Red Army. On April 30 he joined his colleagues of the 1st Byelorussian Front as member of the Forensic Commission under the chairmanship of Dr. Shkaravski. Other members of the Commission were Dr. Anna Yakovlevna Marants,[2] Krayevski's successor in the post of Chief Anatomical Pathologist with the 1st Byelorussian Front (today she works in one of the largest Kiev hospitals), Army Anatomical Pathologist Yuli Valentinovich Gulkevich (now professor in Minsk), and Army Forensic Expert Boguslavski.

I put several questions to Professor Krayevski:

"Where did the autopsy take place?"

"Our base was a field hospital for surgery which had been housed in one of the hospitals of Buch. The autopsy was performed in the mortuary; all the specialized medical instruments were available there, and conditions were entirely normal."

"Who was present during the autopsy?"

"Our Commission, several medics, and the noted Moscow Professor Grazhchenkov, who happened to be in Berlin at the time."

"Did you know whose corpses were being dissected?"

"As far as the Goebbels family and General Krebs were concerned, yes. About the two other corpses there was no precise information, but there was talk that they were probably Hitler and Eva Braun. I repeat, it was mere conjecture."

"When were these two corpses dissected?"

"I believe on May 8."

[2] She herself had been dissecting.

40

Professor Krayevski was right. This date corresponds with that of the report.

The experts' task was both simple and complicated. For professional forensic doctors and anatomical pathologists this was routine work. However, they had to be particularly painstaking. According to the rules for forensic-medical expert opinions, each examination consists of two parts: Evidence and Conclusion. Each part of the report is separately stated and signed, the evidence immediately on the spot, the conclusion after a certain lapse of time. According to Soviet regulations the expert is allowed a delay of up to three days before reaching his final conclusion. If an additional examination, for instance a chemical test, becomes necessary, this period is extended. We shall see that the experts adhered to this procedure, in order to obtain chemical tests, too.[3]

To reproduce the more than fifty pages of the report prepared by Dr. Faust's Commission would be redundant. I here give a summary:

The work of the experts was simplest when it came to the children of Goebbels, since their bodies were not damaged by burning. The same applied to the body of General Krebs. With Krebs as with the six children, the experts detected at the incision of the chest and abdominal cavities "a marked smell of bitter almonds"; the chemical tests of the internal organs established in each case the presence of cyanide compounds.

The medical evidence, incidentally, refutes the statement prevalent in Western historical writing that General Hans Krebs, the last Chief of Staff of the German Field Army, died like a soldier and shot himself with a gun. It is true that the Commission found three lacerated wounds on his head, but these were only superficial injuries, and not bullet entries. The evidence reads: "Death by poisoning with cyanide compounds."[4]

[3] These were performed in Field Laboratory No. 291 of the Army Medical-Epidemiological Service.
[4] No ampule splinters were found in Krebs's mouth. Traces of cyanide compounds were discovered only on examining the internal organs. Krebs must have swallowed the ampule.

41

The corpses of Josef and Magda Goebbels were greatly damaged by burning. In spite of this, traces were found which made it possible to establish the cause of their death. After examination of Goebbels' corpse, the Commission entered into the record:

"Between the teeth of the right lower jaw a splinter of thin colorless glass, belonging to an ampule, was found"; the dissection of the lungs released "a faint smell of bitter almonds"; chemical analysis established the presence of cyanides in the blood and in internal organs. In Magda Goebbels' corpse "splinters from a thin-walled ampule with a blue tip" were found: chemical analysis again established the "presence of cyanide compounds."

The corpses of the two dogs which had been taken from the crater in the Chancellery garden at first did not appear very interesting. One corpse (Document No. 3) was a large German shepherd. On the mucous membrane of the muzzle and of the tongue, "splinters of a thin-walled glass ampule" were detected. The analysis established the presence of cyanide compounds. There were no other injuries. The other corpse—a smaller black dog—had been shot through the head. "No foreign objects were found in the muzzle," was recorded in the autopsy report. Chemical analysis, however, established the "presence of cyanide compounds." The diagnosis: "Death was caused by poisoning with cyanide compounds and by a lethal head injury with extensive destruction of brain matter."

When I asked one of the foremost Soviet forensic doctors, Professor Dr. Vladimir Mikhailovich Smolyaninov, how to interpret such medical evidence, he answered:

"You know, this looks very much like a so-called 'toxicological test.' In the case of the one dog, the ampule had been crushed in its mouth. The other dog had to swallow the ampule and was then shot—with a shot from above, as can be seen from the report."

Professor Smolyaninov's interpretation is confirmed by the recollections of Otto Günsche:

In a hallway of the Führerbunker stood Professor Haase [5] and Sergeant Tornow, the trainer of Hitler's dog. Haase held in his hands an ampule with potassium cyanide and a pair of pliers. Hitler had instructed him to poison the dog "Blondi." Hitler wanted to test the effect of the poison. At midnight, Blondi was poisoned in the toilet. Tornow forced the dog's mouth open, and Haase reached into it, crushing the ampule with the pliers. The poison acted instantly, and soon after Hitler came into the toilet to make sure that Blondi had in fact been poisoned. He did not say a word, his face did not change. A minute later he returned to his study.

The dog mentioned first in the report was Hitler's favorite dog, Blondi. The smaller dog must have been one of those whose killing Günsche describes as follows:

Sergeant Tornow, Hitler's dog trainer, was completely drunk, rushed around in the bunker of the New Chancellery, and shrieked: "The Führer is dead, everyone for himself!"

Panic broke out in the bunker, particularly among the wounded. It soon transpired that Tornow had first shot Blondi's pups, among them Wolf,[6] the dogs of Eva Braun and Frau Christian,[7] and even his own dog.[8]

---

[5] Werner Haase, who substituted at times for Hitler's personal physician, Professor Brandt.
[6] Blondi had whelped five pups in March. Hitler named the most handsome one "Wolf." His prehistory might inspire a satirist: according to Günsche, Blondi was first to be mated to the dog of Frau Troost (the widow of an architect friend of Hitler's). When this misfired, a second "state mating" was arranged, this time with Alfred Rosenberg's dog, which came off. Once, at least, Rosenberg, "Minister for the Occupied Eastern Provinces," was in luck.
[7] Hitler's secretary, wife of the General of the Air Force, Führer Headquarters.
[8] Trevor-Roper reports a similar version: After the poisoning of Blondi, other dogs were shot by a sergeant.

43

10

The text of the final and most important autopsy reports (Documents Nos. 12 and 13) are reproduced verbatim, in the following, either in their entirety or in somewhat abbreviated form:

DOCUMENT NO. 12
concerning the forensic examination of a male corpse disfigured by fire (Hitler's body)

Berlin-Buch, 8.V., 1945
Mortuary CAFS [1] No. 496

The Commission consisting of Chief Expert, Forensic Medicine, 1st Byelorussian Front, Medical Service, Lieutenant Colonel F. I. Shkaravski; Chief Anatomist, Red Army, Medical Service, Lieutenant Colonel N. A. Krayevski; Acting Chief Anatomical Pathologist, 1st Byelorussian Front, Medical Service, Major A. Y. Marants; Army Expert, Forensic Medicine, 3rd Shock Army, Medical Service, Major Y. I. Boguslavski; and Army Anatomical Pathologist, 3rd Shock Army, Medical Service, Major Y. V. Gulkevich, on orders of the member of the Military Council 1st Byelorussian Front, Lieutenant General Telegrin, performed the forensic-medical examination of a male corpse (presumably the corpse of Hitler).

Results of the examination:

A. EXTERNAL EXAMINATION

The remains of a male corpse disfigured by fire were delivered in a wooden box (Length 163 cm., Width 55 cm., Height 53 cm.). On the body was found a piece of yellow jersey, 25 x 8 cm., charred around the edges, resembling a knitted undervest.

In view of the fact that the corpse is greatly damaged, it is

[1] Abbreviation for *Chirurgisches Armeefeldlazarett.*

4 4

difficult to gauge the age of the deceased. Presumably it lies between 50 and 60 years. The dead man's height is 165 cm. (the measurements are approximate since the tissue is charred), the right shinbone measures 39 cm. The corpse is severely charred and smells of burned flesh.

Part of the cranium is missing.[2]

Parts of the occipital bone, the left temporal bone, the lower cheekbones, the nasal bones, and the upper and lower jaws are preserved. The burns are more pronounced on the right side of the cranium than on the left. In the brain cavity parts of the fire-damaged brain and of the dura mater are visible. On face and body the skin is completely missing; only remnants of charred muscles are preserved. There are many small cracks in the nasal bone and the upper jawbones. The tongue is charred, its tip is firmly locked between the teeth of the upper and lower jaws.

In the upper jaw there are nine teeth connected by a bridge of yellow metal (gold). The bridge is anchored by pins on the second left and the second right incisor. This bridge consists of 4 upper incisors (2⌋ 1⌋ ⌊1 ⌊2), 2 canine teeth (3⌋ ⌊3), the first left bicuspid (⌊4), and the first and second right bicuspids (4⌋ 5⌋), as indicated in the sketch. The first left incisor (⌊1) consists of a white platelet, with cracks and a black spot in the porcelain (enamel) at the bottom. This platelet is inset into the visible side of the metal (gold) tooth. The second incisor, the canine tooth, and the left bicuspid, as well as the first and second incisors and the first bicuspid on the right, are the usual porcelain (enamel) dental plates, their posterior parts fastened to the bridge. The right canine tooth is fully capped by yellow metal (gold). The maxillary bridge is vertically sawed off behind the second left bicuspid (⌊5). The lower jawbone lies loose in the singed oral cavity. The alveolar processes are broken in the back and have ragged edges. The front surface and the lower edge of the mandibula

[2] At a somewhat later date occipital parts of a cranium were found, quite probably belonging to Hitler's corpse.

are scorched. On the front surface the charred prongs of dental roots are recognizable. The lower jaw consists of fifteen teeth, ten of which are artificial. The incisors ($\overline{2|}$ $\overline{1|}$ $\overline{|1}$ $\overline{|2}$) and the first right bicuspid ($\overline{4|}$) are natural, exhibiting considerable wear on the masticating surface and considerably exposed necks. The dental enamel has a bluish shimmer and a dirty yellow coloration around the necks. The teeth to the left ($\overline{|4}$, $\overline{|5}$, $\overline{|7}$, and $\overline{|8}$) are artificial, of yellow metal (gold), and consist of a bridge of gold crowns. The bridge is fastened to the third, the fifth (in the bridge, the sixth tooth), and the eighth tooth (in the bridge, the ninth tooth). The second bicuspid to the right ($\overline{5|}$) is topped by a crown of yellow metal (gold) which is linked to the right canine tooth by an arching plate. Part of the masticating surface and the posterior surface of the right canine tooth is capped by a yellow metal (gold) plate as part of the bridge. The first right molar is artificial, white, and secured by a gold clip connected with the bridge of the second bicuspid and the right incisor.

Splinters of glass, parts of the wall and bottom of a thin-walled ampule, were found in the mouth.

The neck muscles are charred, the ribs on the right side are missing, they are burned. The right side of the thorax and the abdomen are completely burned, creating a hole through which the right lung, the liver, and the intestines are open to view. The genital member is scorched. In the scrotum, which is singed but preserved, only the right testicle was found. The left testicle could not be found in the inguinal canal.

The right arm is severely burned, the ends of the bone of the upper arm and the bones of the lower arm are broken and charred. The dry muscles are black and partially brown; they disintegrate into separate fibers when touched. The remnants of the burned part (about two thirds) of the left upper arm are preserved. The exposed end of the bone of the upper arm is charred and protrudes from the dry tissue. Both legs, too, are charred. The soft tissue has in many places disappeared; it is burned and has fallen off. The bones are partially burned and have crumbled. A fracture in the right thighbone and the right shinbone were noted. The left foot is missing.

B. INTERNAL EXAMINATION

The position of the internal organs is normal. The lungs are black on the surface, dark red on the cut surface, and of fairly firm consistence. The mucous membrane of the upper respiratory tracts is dark red. The cardiac ventricles are filled with coagulated reddish-brown blood. The heart muscle is tough and looks like boiled meat. The liver is black on the surface and shows burns; it is of fairly firm consistence and yellowish-brown on the cut surface. The kidneys are somewhat shrunken and measure 9 x 5 x 3.5 cm. Their capsule is easily detachable; the surface of the kidneys is smooth, the pattern effaced, they appear as if boiled. The bladder contains 5 cc. yellowish urine, its mucous membrane is gray. Spleen, stomach, and intestines show severe burns and are nearly black in parts.

NOTE: 1. The following objects taken from the corpse were handed over to the SMERSH Section of the 3rd Shock Army on May 8, 1945: a) a maxillary bridge of yellow metal, consisting of 9 teeth; b) a singed lower jaw, consisting of 15 teeth.

2. According to the record of the interrogation of Frau Käthe Heusermann it may be presumed that the teeth as well as the bridge described in the document are those of Chancellor Hitler.

3. In her talk with Chief Expert of Forensic Medicine, Lieutenant Colonel Shkaravski, which took place on May 11, '45,[3] in the offices of CAFS

[3] I asked N. Krayevski how it was possible for this date to appear in an autopsy report that had been written on May 8. He explained that the report had originally been written by hand; only later was it decided to add the statements of Heusermann. As was mentioned above, the delay between evidence and conclusion is absolutely normal.

47

No. 496, Frau Käthe Heusermann described the state of Hitler's teeth in every detail. Her description tallies with the anatomical data pertaining to the oral cavity of the unknown man whose burned corpse we dissected.

Appended: A test tube with glass splinters from an ampule which were found in the mouth of the body.

signed (Shkaravski)
Chief Expert, Forensic Medicine,
1st Byelorussian Front, Medical Service,
Lieutenant Colonel

signed (Krayevski)
Chief Anatomical Pathologist, Medical Service, Red Army,
Lieutenant Colonel

signed (Marants)
Acting Chief Anatomical Pathologist,
1st Byelorussian Front, Medical Service,
Major

signed (Boguslavski)
Army Expert, Forensic Medicine,
3rd Shock Army, Medical Service,
Major

signed (Gulkevich)
Army Anatomical Pathologist,
3rd Shock Army, Medical Service,
Major

CONCLUSION

Based on the forensic-medical examination of the partially burned corpse of an unknown man and the examination of other corpses from the same group (Documents Nos. 1—11), the Commission reaches the following conclusions:

48

1. *Anatomical characteristics of the body:*
Since the body parts are heavily charred, it is impossible to describe the features of the dead man. But the following could be established:
a) Stature: about 165 cm. (one hundred sixty-five)
b) Age (based on general development, size of organs, state of lower incisors and of the right bicuspid), somewhere between 50 and 60 years (fifty to sixty).
c) The left testicle could not be found either in the scrotum or on the spermatic cord inside the inguinal canal, nor in the small pelvis.
d) The most important anatomical finding for identification of the person are the teeth, with much bridgework, artificial teeth, crowns, and fillings (see documents).

2. *Cause of death:*
On the body, considerably damaged by fire, no visible signs of severe lethal injuries or illnesses could be detected.

The presence in the oral cavity of the remnants of a crushed glass ampule and of similar ampules in the oral cavity of other bodies (see Documents Nos. 1, 2, 3, 5, 6, 8, 9, 10, 11, and 13), the marked smell of bitter almonds emanating from the bodies (Documents Nos. 1, 2, 3, 5, 8, 9, 10, 11), and the forensic-chemical test of internal organs which established the presence of cyanide compounds (Documents Nos. 1, 2, 3, 4, 5, 6, 7, 8, 9, 10, 11) permit the Commission to arrive at the conclusion that death in this instance was caused by poisoning with cyanide compounds.

signed   (Shkaravski)
Chief Expert, Forensic Medicine,
1st Byelorussian Front, Medical Service,
Lieutenant Colonel

signed   (Krayevski)
Chief Anatomical Pathologist, Medical Service, Red Army,
Lieutenant Colonel

signed (Marants)
Acting Chief Anatomical Pathologist,
1st Byelorussian Front, Medical Service,
Major

signed (Boguslavski)
Army Expert, Forensic Medicine,
3rd Shock Army, Medical Service,
Major

signed (Gulkevich)
Army Anatomical Pathologist,
3rd Shock Army, Medical Service,
Major

Thus far the contents of Document No. 12. Before entering into the question of what corpse was being examined—a question left in abeyance in the document—let us consider Document No. 13, which records the results of the forensic-medical examination of a female corpse.[4] The Commission came to the following conclusions:

1. *Anatomical characteristics of the body:*
In view of the fact that the body parts are extensively charred, it is impossible to describe the features of the dead woman. The following, however, could be established:
a) The age of the dead woman lies between 30 and 40 years, evidence of which is also the only slightly worn masticating surface of the teeth.
b) Stature: about 150 cm.
c) The most important anatomical finding for identification of the person are the gold bridge of the lower jaw and its four front teeth.

2. *Cause of death:*
On the extensively charred corpse there were found traces of a splinter injury to the thorax with hemothorax, injuries to

4 For complete text, see Appendix, Document No. 13.

one lung and to the pericardium, as well as six small metal fragments.

Further, remnants of a crushed glass ampule were found in the oral cavity.

In view of the fact that similar ampules were present in other corpses—Documents Nos. 1, 2, 3, 4, 5, 6, 7, 8, 9, 10, 11—that a smell of bitter almonds developed upon dissection —Documents Nos. 1, 2, 3, 4, 5, 6, 7, 8, 9, 10, 11—and based on the forensic-chemical tests of the internal organs of these bodies in which the presence of cyanide compounds was established—Documents Nos. 1, 2, 3, 4, 5, 6, 7, 8, 9, 10, 11 —the Commission reaches the conclusion that notwithstanding the severe injuries to the thorax the immediate cause of death was poisoning by cyanide compounds.

In both cases the experts were faced with the most seriously disfigured of all thirteen corpses. Because of this obstacle to the examination two sentences need to be particularly stressed: "Splinters of glass, parts of the wall and bottom of a thin-walled ampule, were found in the mouth" (Document No. 12)—and "In the oral cavity . . . yellowish glass splinters . . . of a thin-walled ampule were found" (Document No. 13, Appendix). These findings permitted the Commission to come in their summary in both cases to analogous conclusions: Death was caused by poisoning with cyanide compounds.

This conclusion is in no way contradicted by the splinter injuries in Eva Braun's body. These could not possibly have been inflicted on her in the bunker. Most probably they occurred during the burning in the garden, which was under artillery fire. Only shell splinters could have caused the injuries and the hemorrhage in the pleura.

11

Several versions are current concerning the story of the identification of the two corpses, some of them amusingly fictional. A few years ago the German illustrated magazine *Stern* published the account of an M.D., Dr. Arnaudow, a native of Bulgaria, who became a citizen of the West German Republic. He tells in great detail that he was the person who had been able to identify the corpses of Hitler and Frau Braun.

When I showed this account to the actual participants in the identification process, they responded with ironical smiles. Of course they remembered a young Bulgarian student whom they had met on May 9, 1945, at the Charité Hospital. There, Soviet investigators had appeared in search of the Chief of the Throat, Nose, and Ear Clinic, Professor Karl von Eicken, who was known to have treated Hitler for years. The young Bulgarian student offered to accompany the Soviet officers to Kurfürstendamm, where they wanted to track down Hitler's dentist, Professor Blaschke. In those turbulent days this was not an easy task, and Arnaudow acquitted himself honorably. Among the shelled and bombed-out houses he found the intact private office of Blaschke, but not Blaschke himself, who had fled. This ended the Bulgarian's mission.

The moment has come to introduce two Soviet officers who played a signal role in our story. They are Andrei Sevostyanovich Mirozhnichenko, Chief of Counter Intelligence in the 3rd Shock Army, and his deputy, Vasili Ivanovich Gorbushin, two Soviet citizens of the older generation who had been forced by the war to be endlessly on the road. If their biographical data had been exposed to the eyes of a Gestapo investigator, their names would immediately have been singled out for "Special Treatment." As sons of the working class, both were long-standing members of the Communist Party (Mirozhnichenko since 1930, Gorbushin since 1932); they were also officers of the

Cheka [1] (Mirozhnichenko since 1930, Gorbushin since 1938), devoting their lives to combating the enemies of the Soviet State.

At this point in the identification process, Vasili Gorbushin was entrusted with the search for witnesses, assisted by Major Bystrov, an experienced officer with a knowledge of German.

Gorbushin was from Leningrad. In the history of wars, the siege of Leningrad will live on as one of the most cruel and ruthlessly destructive operations. Today, there are voices who wish to excuse it as "military necessity." But at the time no one in Berlin was looking for an excuse for this crime. It was a foregone conclusion that the city bearing Lenin's name would be razed and its population doomed to starvation.

However, the citizens of Leningrad thwarted Hitler's calculations. Vasili Gorbushin, former Chief Foreman of the 2nd Mechanical Division of the famous industrial complex "Krasny Putilovets," survived the worst times of the siege, the winter months of 1941/42. His mission at the time was to counteract the German agents infiltrating the city. From March 1942 he worked in the Volkhov Sector, and from 1943 he was detailed to the Staff of the 3rd Shock Army. On May 9, 1945, Gorbushin's mission was to ascertain whether the corpses found in the garden of the Chancellery were really those of Adolf Hitler and Eva Braun.

Gorbushin's group decided to base their search on the recommendations of the medical investigators. The dissecting doctors had taken into custody jawbones with many artificial bridges, crowns, and fillings. All that was needed for an irrefutable identification were Hitler's dentists. Gorbushin relates:

In the morning of May 9, I went in search of Hitler's dentists. In Professor Blaschke's clinic we were received by a Dr. Bruck. When Bruck learned that we wanted to see his chief on a matter of importance to the Soviet Army Command, he

[1] Abbreviation of Russian for the Soviet Security Service, later replaced by the GPU and eventually by the NKVD.

53

told us that the Professor himself was not at home and asked whether an assistant of the Professor, Käthe Heusermann, might represent him.

I summoned her to an interrogation and had her fetched by the Bulgarian student.

"Where is the medical history on Adolf Hitler's teeth?" I asked Käthe Heusermann.

"Here, in the files," she answered.

Frau Heusermann quickly searched in the file box and pulled out a card which proved to be the medical history of Adolf Hitler. The entries gave evidence that the Führer had had very poor teeth in need of frequent repair.

We also needed the X-ray pictures of Hitler's teeth, but they were not at the clinic. When I asked where they might be, Käthe Heusermann answered that they ought to have been kept in Professor Blaschke's office in the Chancellery.

Wasting no more time in the clinic, we drove to the Chancellery, taking Käthe Heusermann along. Here we went down to the basement, found Professor Blaschke's dental office, and with Käthe Heusermann's assistance soon discovered X-ray photographs of the Führer's teeth and a few gold crowns that had been prepared, but time to put them to use had run out on dentist and patient.

Käthe Heusermann informed me that crowns and bridges for Hitler and Eva Braun had been prepared by a dental technician named Fritz Echtmann, whose address she knew. We found Echtmann at home. I explained the purpose of our visit and asked him to come with us. He was readily willing.

Frau Heusermann and Echtmann were interrogated by me separately. I was assisted by Major Bystrov.

In answer to my questions Käthe Heusermann and Fritz Echtmann described Hitler's teeth from memory in minute detail. Their information about bridges, crowns, and fillings corresponded precisely with the entries in the medical history and with the X-ray pictures that we had found. Next we asked them to identify the jawbones which had been taken from the

54

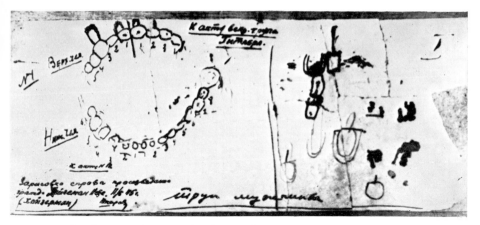

Sketch of Hitler's teeth, drawn by Frau Dr. Heusermann on May 11, 1945

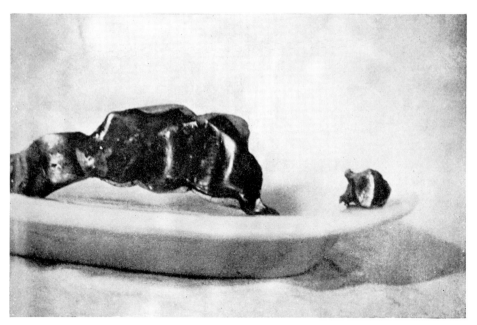

Prosthesis of Eva Braun

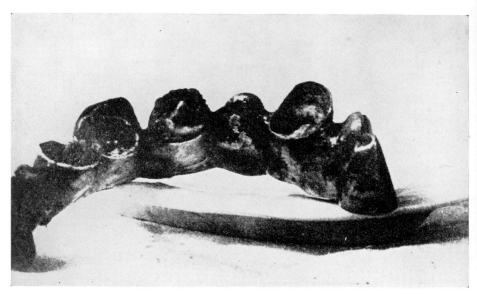

Segment of Hitler's upper teeth   (back view)

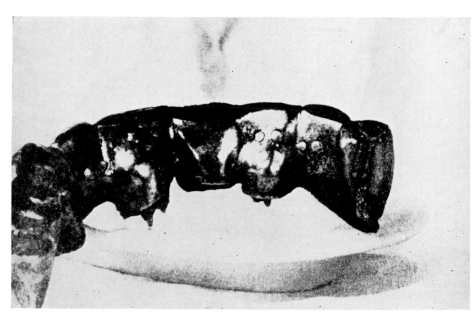

Segment of Hitler's upper teeth   (back view)

Hitler's lower teeth (front view)

Hitler's lower teeth (back view)

Autopsy Commission with (ABOVE) *corpse of General Krebs and* (BELOW) *corpse of Goebbels*

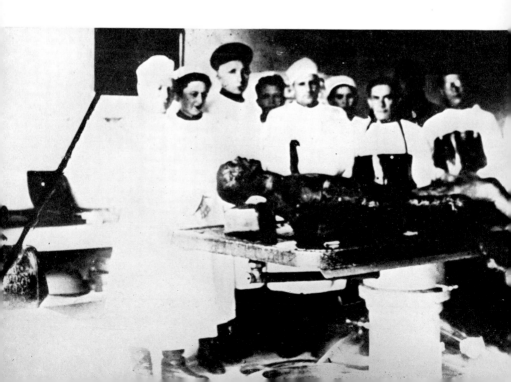

male corpse. Frau Heusermann and Echtmann recognized them unequivocally as those of Adolf Hitler.

In a similar procedure we next asked the dentists to describe Eva Braun's teeth. After they had both answered our questions exhaustively, we placed before them the gold bridge which had been taken from the mouth of the female corpse during the autopsy.

Käthe Heusermann and Fritz Echtmann declared without hesitancy that this prosthesis belonged to Eva Braun. Fritz Echtmann added that the special construction of the bridge prepared for Eva Braun was his own invention and that so far no dental prosthetist had used a similar method of attachment.

Next, our medical experts met again. After examination of the medical history, X-ray pictures, and the jawbone with the teeth of the charred male corpse which had been found on May 4 in the garden of the Chancellery, the experts came to the definite conclusion that these were Adolf Hitler's teeth.

We have every reason to believe in the trustworthiness of Gorbushin's account, since it has received documentary confirmation: the subsequently drawn up records of the interrogation. On May 9 Professor Eicken was interrogated by Colonel Mirozhnichenko and Gorbushin. Frau Heusermann was repeatedly interrogated, on May 10 by Gorbushin himself.[2] Here is the crucial part of the interrogation:

Question: Can you establish from the dental bridges that they belong to Hitler?
Answer: Yes, there is no doubt of it.
Question: We have shown you the dental bridge of an upper jaw and a lower jaw with teeth. Do you know to whom these teeth belong?
Answer: The teeth shown to me belong to the German Chan-

[2] Yelena Rshevskaya, who in 1965 published a report on the search for the leaders of the Third Reich, was interpreter during this interrogation. Cf. Yelena Rshevskaya, *Hitlers Ende ohne Mythos* (Berlin, 1967), pp. 90 ff.

cellor Adolf Hitler. The upper jaw on the left, behind the fourth tooth, exhibits a distinct trace which occurred when the gold bridge was sawed by the dental drill, at the time of the extraction of the sixth tooth. This extraction was performed by Professor Blaschke with my assistance in the autumn. . . .

All further evidence that these bridges are Adolf Hitler's tallies with those named by me before from memory, with the exception of the fourth lower right tooth, which I believed to be an artificial porcelain tooth. But the teeth you have shown me prove that this tooth is a natural one.

Question: Can you affirm that the teeth shown to you are Adolf Hitler's teeth?

Answer: Yes, I affirm that the teeth shown to me are Adolf Hitler's teeth.

The dental technician Fritz Echtmann confirmed Frau Heusermann's statements on May 11.[3] On the same day, Frau Heusermann was interrogated by Dr. Faust Shkaravski. Here are his recollections:

On May 11, 1945, Hitler's medical history was sent to me from the aforementioned Field Hospital for Surgery, No. 496 in Buch. Käthe Heusermann, an assistant of Hitler's stomatologist, Professor Blaschke, was also brought to me. She had helped to prosthesize Hitler's teeth in her capacity as specialist in stomatology. I remember very clearly how frightened she was during the interrogation. However, the interrogation proceeded very smoothly, really like an ordinary conversation between doctors. I, a Soviet physician, was speaking with a German doctor. In the course of our conversation, which lasted between two and three hours, Frau Heusermann gladly ate some of our candy. Her fear soon evaporated. She de-

---

[3] Later, as a Soviet prisoner, Echtmann produced sketches and descriptions of the jaws of Eva Braun, whose dental prostheses were made by him, and of those of Hitler, on whose dental prosthesis he collaborated.

scribed minutely the specific features of Hitler's dental prostheses and drew them with her own hand. I even started to argue with her, because I had overlooked one detail when examining the teeth and had miscounted the steel pins. She turned out to be right.

Having finished with the theoretical part of our conversation, we proceeded to the practical part, that is, I wanted to check the correctness of her statements against the prostheses themselves, which were in my desk. I took them out and placed them before Frau Heuscrmann. Frau Heusermann repeated everything again in detail and declared categorically that the prosthesis I had shown her was in fact Hitler's dental prosthesis. The picture was clear beyond doubt, for Frau Heusermann as well as for me as forensic expert.

After the interrogation of Frau Heusermann and Echtmann the forensic experts no longer doubted the identity of the corpses. I asked Professor Krayevski which detail of this memorable experts' report he remembered most clearly.

"Probably the smell of bitter almonds, which we all noticed. For an anatomical pathologist or a forensic physician this smell says unmistakably: Poisoning by cyanide compounds."

I further mentioned to Professor Krayevski one particular detail which had been established at the dissection of Hitler's internal organs: the missing second testicle. In medical parlance this defect is known as monorchism. Krayevski remarked that monorchism is a fairly frequent phenomenon and as a rule is congenital: such a defect did not exclude a normal sexual life. I asked whether this might be the consequence of an illness. Himmler is said to have told Dr. Kersten that Hitler in his early years had contracted syphilis. According to Professor Krayevski, however, there is no connection between syphilis and monorchism.

This congenital defect of Hitler's had not been mentioned anywhere in the existing literature. But Professor Hans Karl von Hasselbach, one of Hitler's physicians, remembers that the

Führer always refused categorically to have a medical check-up.[4] It is conceivable that this refusal was motivated by this physical abnormality.

Hitler died in the firm conviction that all traces of his physical existence had been destroyed. But Soviet shells and the unbearable smell of burning corpses kept his subordinates from following through in the execution of the Führer's last commands. Thus it became possible that the last (forensic-medical) opinion on Hitler was pronounced by Dr. Shkaravski, by Dr. Faust. Once upon a time Germany's greatest poet raised the name of Faust to a symbol of the triumph of human reason. Once again reason triumphed over madness.

Having concluded their work, the Commission under Dr. Shkaravski submitted its findings to the Military Council of the 1st Byelorussian Front.

12

Anne Frank was a child. Maria Rolnikaite, who was imprisoned in the Warsaw ghetto and left notes of similar impact, was also only fourteen years old. Among the victims of Babi Yar, of Lidice, there were many children—and a great many perished in Dresden.

These few signposts may serve as a yardstick as we turn to the murder of the six Goebbels children. Six, it may be said, are not six hundred thousand. But murder is always murder. And even those historians who appraise the life of the former Reich Minister for Propaganda and National Enlightenment with an unprejudiced eye will not dare to affirm that Helga (born September 1, 1932), Hilde (April 13, 1934), Helmut (October 2, 1935), Holde (February 2, 1937), Hedda (May 5, 1938), and Heide (October 29, 1940) willingly chose their death.

In the chaos of events around May 1, 1945, the fate of these

[4] Cf. H. D. Röhrs, *Hitlers Krankheit* (Neckargmünd, 1966), p. 71.

58

children escaped proper attention. But the example of the Goebbels family throws an appalling light on the abyss to which horror propaganda can lead even its perpetrators. Did Goebbels and his wife seriously believe that the Allies would wreak their vengeance on six children? The postwar period has refuted such conjectures. Not a hair was harmed on the heads of the children of Bormann, Himmler, Göring, and many other Party bigwigs.

Not everything can be explained by a fanaticism which knows no bounds. But a regime which welcomes murder as the means of self-assertion must in the long run damage its own soul. Whoever ceases to respect his neighbor as a human being will in the end cease to be a human being himself. His biographer Helmut Heiber believes that Goebbels wanted to put himself in the spotlight through the death of his children, to create for himself an aura, a legend, conducive to immortality, to surround his end with the "awe-inspiring grandeur of antiquity and a sense of fateful doom." [1]

How were Goebbels' children murdered? Opinions differ. Some, among them Goebbels' erstwhile Secretary of State Werner Naumann, assert that Magda Goebbels herself did the deed. Another version has it that their mother waited outside while the doctors administered poison to the children. Still others believe that we shall never know exactly what the actual proceedings were.

I do not wish to assert that the following documents throw a full light on the events. But they have one advantage: they were drawn up immediately after these events. The reader will notice that the eyewitness Dr. Helmut Kunz did not at first come out with the full truth. Then the Soviet Court of Inquiry subjected him again to a probing cross-examination.

RECORD OF INTERROGATION

May 7, 1945. Lieutenant Colonel Vasilyev, Chief of Counter Intelligence, 4th Section, SMERSH, 1st Byelorussian Front, has

[1] Helmut Heiber, *Joseph Goebbels* (Munich, 1965), p. 370.

59

interrogated the prisoner of war of the German Armed Forces, *Helmut Kunz*, with interrogating magistrate Senior Lieutenant Vlassov as translator into and out of the German.

Personal information: Kunz, Helmut Gustavovich, born 1910 in Ettlingen/Baden, dentist, lately adjutant of the Chief Physician, Medical Administration of the SS, in the Chancellery. As of April 21, '45, his medical section was disbanded and he was transferred to a military hospital. Upon the evacuation of the hospital from Berlin on April 23, he was detailed to the Chancellery. At that period, there was no dentist there.

Question: Were you, up to April 23 of this year, in any way connected with the Chancellery?

Answer: Up to that date I was in no way connected with the Chancellery.

Question: What is your rank?

Answer: SS-Sturmbannführer.

Question: Whom did you personally attend during your activity in the Chancellery?

Answer: I personally attended Frau Goebbels and later also the soldiers detailed to the Chancellery.

Question: How long have you known Goebbels and his family?

Answer: I came to know Goebbels on May 1 of this year through his wife. Up to that date I knew him only from his speeches in public broadcasts.

Question: How did it happen that you, without previous access to the Chancellery, were introduced to Goebbels on May 1 of this year and immediately permitted access to his apartment?

Answer: Probably because I treated Frau Goebbels.

Question: Have you been in Goebbels' apartment?

Answer: I was in the bunker, in the Chancellery, where his family also were lodged—his wife and his children.

Question: What physical defects do you know of in Goebbels, his wife, and his children?

60

Answer: His wife and children were completely normal; Goebbels had a limp in his right leg.

Question: Tell us more explicitly what happened to Goebbels and his family.

Answer: On April 27 of this year I met Frau Goebbels after dinner between 8 and 9 P.M. in the hallway at the entrance to Hitler's bunker. She told me that she wanted to speak to me about a highly important matter and added that the situation had reached the point where we would probably have to die. She therefore asked me to help her kill the children. I agreed.

After this conversation Frau Goebbels led me to the children's bedroom and showed me all her children. The children were preparing to go to bed, and I did not speak to any of them.

As the children were getting into their beds, Goebbels came in, wished the children a good night, and disappeared again.

I spent another 10 to 15 minutes in the room, then Frau Goebbels dismissed me and I returned to my office, which was in one of the bunkers, approximately 500 meters' distance from the bunker where Hitler, Goebbels, and the other persons attached to Führer Headquarters lived.

On May 1 of this year, Frau Goebbels telephoned me somewhere between 4 and 5 P.M. She said that time was running out and asked me to come immediately to her bunker. I went over but did not take any drugs along. As I entered Goebbels' apartment, I saw in the study Goebbels himself, his wife, the Secretary of State of the Propaganda Ministry, Naumann, who were debating something.

I waited about 10 minutes in front of the study, until Goebbels and Naumann left. Frau Goebbels then asked me to come in and told me that the decision was made (this referred to the killing of the children), the Führer had died already, and the troops would try to break out between 8 and

9 P.M. Consequently we would have to die, there was no other way.

In the course of our talk I offered Frau Goebbels to send the children to the hospital and put them under the protection of the Red Cross. But she did not agree to this and said that it would be better for the children to die.

After about 20 minutes, while we were still talking, Goebbels returned to his study and turned to me with the words: "Doctor, I would be most grateful if you could help my wife to put the children to sleep."

I repeated to Goebbels what I had offered his wife, to provide shelter for the children at the hospital and to put them under the protection of the Red Cross. But he answered: "That's not possible; after all, they are the children of Goebbels!"

Goebbels then left and I stayed with his wife, who spent about an hour consulting cards.

After about an hour Goebbels came back to us, accompanied by the deputy Gauleiter of Berlin, Schacht. I gathered from their conversation that Schacht was to try to break out with the soldiers. He took leave of Goebbels. Goebbels gave him a pair of glasses with dark horn rims and said: "Take this as a memento, these are the glasses the Führer used to wear." Then Schacht said good-by to Frau Goebbels and to me and left.

After Schacht had gone, Frau Goebbels said: "Our troops are withdrawing, the Russians may be here any minute and break in on us. We'll have to act quickly."

As we left the study, that is, I and Frau Goebbels, two young persons in uniform, unknown to me, were sitting in the antechamber; one wore the uniform of the Hitler Youth, I can't remember how the other was dressed. Goebbels and his wife said good-by to the two, and one of the strangers asked: "And what is your decision, Herr Minister?" Goebbels did not answer, but his wife declared: "The Gauleiter of Berlin and his family are staying in Berlin and will die here."

62

Having said good-by to these persons, Goebbels went back into his study and I went with his wife to their bunker apartment. In the hall Frau Goebbels took a syringe filled with morphine from the cabinet and gave it to me. We then entered the children's bedroom; the children were already in bed but not yet asleep.

Frau Goebbels said to the children: "Children, don't be afraid, the doctor is going to give you an injection, a kind that is now given to all children and soldiers." With these words she left the room. I stayed behind by myself and injected the morphine, beginning with the two older girls and then going on to the boy and the other girls.

I made the injections into the underarm below the elbow, 0.5 cc. for each, in order to make the children sleepy. The injecting lasted about 8 to 10 minutes, then I went back into the hall, where I met Frau Goebbels. I told her that we would have to wait about 10 minutes for the children to fall asleep. At the same time I looked at my watch. It was 8:40 P.M. (on May 1). After 10 minutes Frau Goebbels went with me into the children's bedroom, where she stayed about 5 minutes placing in the mouth of each child a crushed ampule containing potassium cyanide. (Each glass ampule contained 1.5 cc. of potassium cyanide.) As we returned to the hall, she said: "This is the end."

I now went down with her to Goebbels' study, where we found him in a very nervous state, pacing back and forth in the room. As we entered the study Frau Goebbels said: "It's over with the children, now we have to think of ourselves." Goebbels answered: "We have to hurry, there's not much time left." Then Frau Goebbels said: "We don't want to die here in the bunker," and Goebbels added: "Of course not, we'll go into the garden." His wife answered: "Not into the garden, to the Wilhelmsplatz, where you worked all your life." [The Wilhelmsplatz is situated between the Ministry of Propaganda and the Chancellery.]

During the conversation Goebbels thanked me for having

63

helped ease their burden, then he said good-by to me, wishing me success in life and a safe return home. I then went to my hospital (it was now 10:15 or 10:20 P.M.).

Question: Where could Frau Goebbels obtain poison (potassium cyanide)?

Answer: Frau Goebbels told me herself that she had received the morphine and the syringe from Stumpfegger, Hitler's second physician.[2] Whom she got the ampules with potassium cyanide from, I do not know. . . .

Question: Were you the only one to participate in the killing of Goebbels' children?

Answer: Yes, I was the only one.

Kunz was soon interrogated again. Here are extracts from the record drawn up by Interrogating Magistrate Vlassov on May 19:

Question: . . . The examining authorities have received information that Dr. Stumpfegger assisted you in the killing of Goebbels' children. Can you confirm this?

Answer: Yes, I admit that I made mistaken statements about the circumstances of the children's killing. It is true that I was aided by Dr. Stumpfegger. The precise circumstances of the killing of Goebbels' children were as follows:

After I had injected morphine into all the children I went from the children's bedroom into the adjacent room and waited there with Frau Goebbels until the children had fallen asleep. She asked me to help her adminster the poison to the children. I refused, telling her that I didn't have the fortitude to do this. Then Frau Goebbels asked me to fetch Dr. Stumpfegger, Hitler's first assistant physician. After three or four minutes I found Stumpfegger, who was sitting in the dining room of Hitler's bunker, and said to him: "Doctor, Frau Goebbels wants you to come to her." As I returned with

---

[2] Dr. Ludwig Stumpfegger, purported to have been killed during the last attempt to break out of the Chancellery.

Stumpfegger into the hall of the children's bedroom, where I had left Frau Goebbels, she was no longer there, and Stumpfegger immediately went into the bedroom. I waited next door. Four or five minutes later Stumpfegger came back with Frau Goebbels from the children's bedroom; he left immediately without saying a word to me. Frau Goebbels did not speak either, she only wept.

I accompanied her to the lower story of the bunker and came to Goebbels' study, where I said good-by to both and then went to my hospital.

Question: Why were you silent about Dr. Stumpfegger's participation during the previous interrogations?

Answer: The events of the last days before the surrender of the German garrison in Berlin had shocked me so deeply that I plainly and unintentionally overlooked this circumstance.

So far Dr. Kunz. As Stumpfegger is supposed to be dead, it is difficult to check Kunz's statements. The outcome, however, is known. Dr. Shkaravski has set it down in documents Nos. 1-2 and 8-11 concerning the examination of the children's corpses. The documents drawn up on May 7 and 8 in Buch are sufficiently similar for a summary of "Document No. 1, concerning the forensic-medical examination of the corpse of an unknown girl," to suffice here. (The girl is the twelve-year-old Helga Goebbels.)

CONCLUSION

Based on the forensic-medical autopsy of the corpse of a girl approximately fifteen years old [3] and the forensic-medical examination of her internal organs, the Commission has reached the following conclusions:

1. The autopsy revealed no injuries or pathological changes which might have caused the death of the dead girl.

2. In the mouth, splinters of a crushed glass ampule were found; upon dissection of the corpse a pronounced smell of

[3] The experts estimated the age from the appearance of the body. A miscalculation of one or two years is permissible in such cases.

65

bitter almond was perceived, and the chemical test of the internal organs established the presence of cyanide compounds.

This leads to the conclusion that the death of the approximately fifteen-year-old girl was caused by poisoning by a cyanide compound.

13

The circumstances of the death of Hitler, Goebbels, and others had been thoroughly examined by the medical experts. An important stage had drawn to a close. Moscow was immediately informed of the results, which, however, were not published. Why? Not because of doubts as to the credibility of the experts. By the end of May their conclusions were submitted to the highest Command of the State and the Army, which recognized the medical examination as final; the corpses therefore were now completely burned and their ashes strewn to the wind.

There is no doubt that Y. V. Stalin showed considerable interest in the fate of Hitler. G. K. Zhukov remembers that Stalin frequently inquired about him and indicated that investigations should be continued. Marshal Zhukov mentioned this at the international press conference which he held in June 1945 in Berlin.

Was Y. V. Stalin so skeptical because he did not wish to accept the fact that Hitler had "escaped" his just punishment? Those who were involved in the investigation remember that other considerations played a far larger role. First, it was resolved not to publish the results of the forensic-medical report but to "hold it in reserve" in case someone might try to slip into the role of "the Führer saved by a miracle." Secondly, it was resolved to continue the investigations in order to exclude any possibility of error or deliberate deception.

For this purpose the information gathered in Berlin was not enough. It had to be compared with other data. As the Soviet investigating authorities had at their disposal a great many people who had stayed in the bunker of the Chancellery, they were interrogated with the purpose of finding out *whether Hitler would have been physically able to flee Berlin at the time.*

We know today that this caution was completely justified. In the last days of the battle for Berlin quite a few people were able to escape from the air-raid bunker of the Chancellery. Hanna Reitsch, the aviator, was able to start with her plane from the Ost-West-Achse [1] as late as April 28. Reich Youth Leader Arthur Axmann and Secretary of State Walter Naumann succeeded in giving all Soviet control barriers the slip, not to mention Reichsleiter Martin Bormann and Gestapo Chief Heinrich Müller, whose further fate is not known even today. Heinrich Himmler had false papers issued for himself, and only by accident did he fall into the hands of the English. A man as widely known as the Gauleiter for East Prussia and Reich Commissar for the Ukraine, Erich Koch, could live in hiding in West Germany until 1950.

The Soviet investigating magistrates interrogated primarily the following persons about Hitler's fate: his adjutant Otto Günsche, his pilot Hans Baur, the chief of Hitler's bodyguard, SS-Brigadeführer Johann Rattenhuber, and the Combat Commander, SS-Brigadeführer Wilhelm Mohnke. They were interrogated for the first time immediately after having been taken prisoners. Understandably, these interrogations were rather cursory. At the time it was not yet known that Heinz Linge, Hitler's valet, who had witnessed the last minutes of Hitler's life, would be apprehended.

Linge's story is not without irony. First he had blended into the mass of prisoners of war, hoping to remain unnoticed. In this hope he slipped his watch to an unknown woman who was standing by the roadside as the prisoners were led through the streets of Berlin. The watch was inscribed with Hitler's name. But Linge had miscalculated: the woman reported her find to the Soviet Military Command, which immediately ordered an

[1] A throughway in Berlin.

intensive search for Heinz Linge among the many thousands of prisoners in Berlin. The search was successful.

During interrogations the examining magistrate concentrated on two questions:

First: To what extent did Hitler have the theoretical and practical possibility of escaping from Berlin?

Second: To what extent are the statements about Hitler's suicide to be believed, and if it happened how did it happen?

The exhaustive interrogations (there were even scheduled court sessions to which witnesses were summoned) resulted in many volumes of transcripts which cannot be reproduced in the framework of this account. The conclusion arrived at was:

First: Hitler was able to leave Berlin by air until April 28.

Second: Most of the inhabitants of the Führerbunker tried in every way to talk Hitler into escaping.

Third: Hitler did not follow this advice.

Almost all the people in Hitler's entourage knew that they would not be able to escape death in the Chancellery. There were tragicomic scenes: Morell, his personal physician, sobbingly implored Hitler to allow him to leave Berlin. Everybody entreated Hitler to remove himself to the alpine National Redoubt. The pilot Baur even offered to fly the Führer to Manchukuo! But Hitler's physical disintegration and his demoralization had advanced to such a point that he could no longer contemplate leaving the bunker. After April 20 he no longer dared venture into daylight, and the explosions of the Russian shells made him shudder.

Hitler did not leave Berlin. Only one question now remained unanswered: By what means did Hitler commit suicide?

14

The saying goes that the bigger a lie the more likely it is to be believed. The Nazi regime gave evidence of how quite literally the entire existence of a State can be based on deception. Even Hitler's death is surrounded by a fabric of lies.

The biggest was the official lie, the news circulated on May 1 by the few still operating radio stations of the German Reich: that the Führer Adolf Hitler had died a soldier's death at his command post in the Chancellery. It appears that, big though it was, very few people fell for this lie. At any rate no one in our circles believed this news.

Then, little by little, the news came through that Hitler had shot himself. This version has maintained itself in various memoirs and also in numerous historical research works.

One of the first German researchers who questioned this version was Erich Kuby, in his book *Die Russen in Berlin 1945*. In his analysis of the various testimonies he established many variants, and some, even if unimportant ones, in Soviet publications.[1]

Kuby came fairly close to the heart of the question in his article for *Der Spiegel:* "It was in the interests of the Führer's entourage that the idol of the Third Reich should end his life by shooting himself courageously with a gun." But in the same place Kuby inserts a proviso: "It was just as much in the interests of the Soviet side that Hitler should have poisoned himself like a coward. Both sides had weighty reasons to hide the truth."

Kuby probably wanted to be impeccably objective. But it is obvious that his thesis lacks logic. If he were right, the Soviet side would long ago have made an official declaration that Hitler poisoned himself. But this was not done—quite the contrary. Up

[1] Kuby accepted with some skepticism the statements of the Soviet interpreter Yelena Rzhevskaya, with whom he spoke in Moscow. He noticed that she was unable to describe precisely the location of the house in which Hitler's corpse was examined forensically. As the conversation between Kuby and Mrs. Rzhevskaya took place in my Moscow office, I can name the reasons for her uncertainty (which Kuby virtually interpreted as one of the specific qualities of Russian mentality). The vagueness of her wording has a simple explanation: in those very March days of 1965 an article by Yelena Rzhevskaya on the Berlin events was prepared for publication in the magazine *Znamya*. For this reason the author wanted to keep certain information for herself. Mrs. Rzhevskaya, by the way, was not present at the autopsy.

69

to a certain time some Soviet publications also mention the version of suicide by shooting.[2] This on the one hand. On the other hand we have no interest whatsoever in "hiding the truth," rather we want to discover the truth.

What is to be said for Hitler's poisoning himself?

First: The medical report. It is unequivocal.

Second: The identification procedure.

Third: The analysis of the circumstances of the suicide.

During the investigation in Moscow, the various statements on the actual time of the suicide resulted in curious ambiguities. Those who ought to have known and remembered could not remember and ignored the most crucial facts. This is particularly true with regard to the depositions of Günsche and Linge, though both these men were bound to know more than the others. Actually they did not contribute to the clarification of the matter even after they were released.

Let us take a close look at Linge's report as it was published in *Der Spiegel,* No. 22, 1965. Linge asserts that Hitler and Eva Braun, after taking leave of their entourage, entered the room where they wanted to take their lives on April 30, at about 3 P.M. The valet, after closing the door, purports to have run up the stairs in complete confusion and, on the point of stepping outside, to have gone down again because he could hear the bursting of Soviet shells nearby. As he again came close to the door of the room, he opened it slightly and smelled gunpowder. Thereupon he fetched Bormann and both entered the room together. Linge asserts that Hitler and Eva Braun were sitting at opposite ends of the sofa which stood against the wall. On the table in front of Hitler lay a Walther pistol caliber 7.65. Another pistol (caliber 6.35) was lying on the floor in front of Hitler. The bullet entry could be seen in Hitler's left temple, but not a single drop of blood had been drawn. Linge concludes from all this that Hitler shot himself in the left temple with the left hand.

[2] For instance, G. L. Rozanov in his work on the annihilation of Fascist Germany, published in 1961.

70

Goebbels' corpse

А К Т № 12.

судебно-медицинского исследования обго<del>рев</del>шего трупа
мужчины /предположительно труп Гитлера/.

8 мая 1945 года город БЕРЛИН- Бух.<del>Морг</del> ХППГ № 496.
комиссия в составе главного судебно-медицинского эксперта
I-го Белорусского фронта - подполковника медицинской службы
ШКАРАВСКОГО Ф.И. , главного патолого-анатома Красной Армии
подполковника медицинской службы КРАЕВСКОГО Н.А., И.О. Главного патолого-анатома I-го Белорусского фронта - майора
медицинской службы МАРАНЦ А.Я., армейского суд.мед.эксперта
3 Ударной Армии - майора медицинской службы БОГУСЛАВСКОГО
Ю.И. и армейского патолого-анатома 3 Ударной Армии - майора
медицинской службы ГУЛЬКЕВИЧ Ю.В. по приказанию Члена Воен-
ного Совета I-го Белорусского фронта генерал-лейтенанта
ТЕЛЕГИНА от 3 мая 1945 года- произвела судебно-медицинское
исследование трупа мужчины /предположительно труп ГИТЛЕРА/

  При исследовании обнаружено:

  А. Наружный осмотр.

    В деревянном ящике длиной 163 см., шириной 55см. и
высиной 53 см. доставлены остатки обгоревшего трупа мужчины.
На трупе был обнаружен обгоревший по краям кусок трикотажной
материи размером 25 х 8 см., желтоватого цвета, похожий на
трикотажную рубашку.

    В виду того, что труп обгорел, судить о возрасте трудно,
можно предположить, что возраст был около 50-60 лет, рост
его 165 см./измерение неточно, вследствие обугливания тканей/,

Autopsy report on Hitler (first page)

- позволяет придти комиссии к заключению, что в данном
случае смерть наступила в результате отравления цианистыми
соединениями. /~~подчеркнуто~~/.

ГЛАВНЫЙ СУД МЕД ЭКСПЕРТ I БФ
ПОДПОЛКОВНИК М.С.   /ШКАРАВСКИЙ/

ГЛАВНЫЙ ПАТОЛОГО-АНАТОМ КРАСНОЙ АРМИИ
ПОДПОЛКОВНИК М.С.
                                     /КРАЕВСКИЙ/

И.О. ГЛАВНОГО ПАТОЛОГО-АНАТОМА I БФ
М А Й О Р М.С.
                                     /МАРАНЦ/

СУД МЕД ЭКСПЕРТ 3 УДАРНОЙ АРМИИ
М А Й О Р М.С.
                                     /БОГУСЛАВСКИЙ/

ПАТОЛОГО-АНАТОМ 3 УДАРНОЙ АРМИИ
М А Й О Р М.С.
                                     /ГУЛЬКЕВИЧ/

4 экз.

Autopsy report on Hitler (last page)

Corpses of Goebbels' children and of General Krebs at Plötzensee

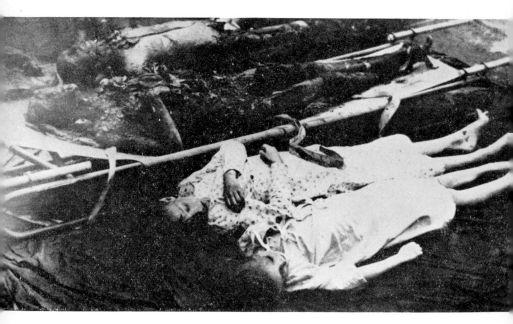

Corpses of Goebbels, his wife, and two of their children

Erich Kuby, who repeated Linge's tale, himself had the same grave doubts that we have. First, the assumption that Hitler shot himself with his left hand is unlikely: he was not left-handed. Second, his hands, including the left, trembled greatly—Hitler's left hand more strongly than the right—and this they did even before the assassination attempt of July 20, 1944. We cannot avoid adding that Linge changed his version after the publication in *Der Spiegel:* in the later version it was not the left but the right temple! A "synopsis" of the various accounts which appeared from time to time gives an entertaining picture:

	Günsche (1950)	*Günsche* (1960)	*Linge*
Position of the bodies of Hitler and Braun	Sitting next to each other on the sofa	Hitler in chair, sitting, Braun lying in chair	Sitting at opposite ends of sofa (Braun left)
Entry of shot in Hitler	Right temple	No particulars	Left temple

	Kempka	*Shirer Trevor-Roper*	*Bullock*
Position of the bodies of Hitler and Braun	On sofa (Hitler lying, Braun sitting)	Lying next to each other on sofa	Lying next to each other (Braun right)
Entry of shot in Hitler	Mouth	Mouth	Mouth

The confusion and lack of uniformity in the statements indicate that the collaborators of Hitler who managed to escape from the bunker purposely tried to hide the truth in order to foster the legend that the Führer had shot himself like a man.

All the same, the Moscow investigations also examined the hypothesis of the shooting. The theory that Hitler might have shot himself first and then taken poison was excluded from the start. The reverse order seemed unlikely. Cyanide acts instantly, and it is therefore hardly conceivable that a person who crushed an ampule of poison in his mouth would also be able to pull a trigger. I inquired of the foremost Soviet forensic scientist, Professor Dr. Vladimir Mikhailovich Smolyaninov, whether he had knowledge of any such cases. In his entire working career he had not come across a single instance. This method would in any case require a strong will, lightning reactions, and a steady hand. But we know how severely Hitler's hands shook. His state of health, moreover, excluded such a possibility.[3]

A third variant proposed that somebody had shot Hitler after he took the poison—for safety's sake, as it were.

There exist a number of indirect yet important testimonies according to which Hitler himself had voiced the idea of shooting. In a recently published book by Berin E. Gun on Eva Braun, which is based on the reports of close relatives and of Hitler's secretaries Junge, Christian, Wolf, and Schröder, Gun quotes the following remark, which Hitler made at a conference during which the possibility of armed resistance against the Russians was discussed. Hitler said:

"I can no longer hold a rifle, I would break down in the first hours, and who would then give me the *coup de grâce?*"

This he followed up with a lengthy discourse to the effect that he did not wish to become a living exhibit in the Moscow Zoo. Obviously, he was not particularly imaginative; he had a morbid fear of becoming an exhibit, rather than a rational fear of having to face a tribunal.

On April 29, the suicide theme recurs between Hitler and Krebs. Krebs said:

[3] According to J. Recktenwald, *Woran hat Adolf Hitler gelitten?* (Munich, 1963), all symptoms point to advanced Parkinson's disease.

72

"The best way would be to shoot oneself in the mouth."
Hitler answered:

"Of course, but who would finish me off if my wound wasn't mortal? And I could never bring myself to shoot Eva."

Who, indeed, would have shot him?

In Hitler's immediate entourage there were Adjutant Günsche, valet Linge, Chief of the Bodyguard Rattenhuber, pilot Baur, and Reichsleiter Bormann. The Soviet examining magistrates tend to assume that a man as cowardly as Bormann would hardly have committed such a deed. In those days, Bormann still harbored the hope of rescuing the Third Reich and becoming one of its chief representatives; for this reason alone he would have found it inexpedient to shoot the Führer. Rattenhuber's personal traits also exclude such an assumption in his case.

Might it have been done by Hitler's pilot Baur? According to other testimony, he was much too preoccupied with another important matter when Hitler ended his life: he tried to hide a present he had received from Hitler. Hitler had willed the pilot his favorite portrait of Frederick the Great, and Baur tried all kinds of tricks to preserve the portrait: in fact he detached the canvas from the frame, rolled it around a walking stick, and hid it behind his back.

The attention of the Soviet examining magistrates was aroused by the testimony of SS-Brigadeführer Mohnke. Taken prisoner, he stated during his interrogation that he had heard as early as April 30 about Hitler's "self-poisoning." As the persons who knew about it he named Goebbels, Bormann, Burgdorf, Krebs, and Rattenhuber. Three of these are dead, one is missing. Rattenhuber was taken prisoner by the Soviets. He prepared a report about the last days in the Chancellery on May 20, 1945, fairly soon after the events. The entry concerning April 30 reads:

About 1 A.M. I got up again, checked the guards, and arrived about 4 A.M. in the Führerbunker. Here, Linge informed me that the Führer . . . had committed suicide and that he

73

[Linge] had executed the most difficult order in his life. I knew from Dr. Stumpfegger that he had had to procure potassium cyanide for the Führer and his wife.

Though Hitler had taken leave of me, I was completely shattered by Linge's news. I sat down in a chair and Linge told me that the corpses had been wrapped in blankets and burned near the emergency exit in the garden. He also told me that there was a blood spot on the carpet; as I looked at him with astonishment, knowing that Hitler had taken potassium cyanide, he told me that Hitler had ordered him to leave the room and to re-enter it ten minutes later, once everything was quiet, and to execute his order. I told Linge that I knew what he meant about "the most difficult order" when he placed Hitler's pistol on the table of the antechamber.

In his later depositions, Rattenhuber stated that there was one more person who knew of "the most difficult order." This was his deputy, Kriminalkommissar Hoegl. According to Rattenhuber, Hoegl had also been told by Linge that he had to execute such an order. Rattenhuber: "I came to the conclusion that Hitler did not entirely trust the effect of the poison on his organism and therefore ordered his valet Linge to go into his room after a certain lapse of time and shoot him." [4]

Such a request cannot be considered entirely senseless. It is known that certain chemical substances (for instance, basic compounds) exert a neutralizing effect on cyanide compounds.[5] During the war Hitler had taken enormous quantities of various drugs which Dr. Morell prescribed for him. And the fear that he might one day get into "the Russian waxworks" was so strong in him that he tried the effect of the cyanide ampule first on his dog.

While Rattenhuber believed that Linge had fired the fatal shot, Soviet researchers are of the opinion that it was Günsche

[4] Rattenhuber's deposition of November 15, 1951, set down in Russian, read to the witness, and then signed by him.
[5] One such case in the history of forensic medicine is notorious: Rasputin did not react to cyanide because he was an alcoholic.

who pulled the trigger. One thing in any case is certain: If a shot was fired in the closed room, it was not the shot that should bear testimony to the manly decision of the "Gröfaz," the "greatest military commander of all times." [6] It would not even be metaphorical to say that Hitler "was killed like a dog"— killed in the same manner as the dog that also was first poisoned and then shot.

Professor Smolyaninov, with whom I discussed the conjectural suicide, asserted that for him, as a forensic scientist, all conjectures about shots were inconclusive. According to the forensic anatomical-pathological evidence, the cause of Hitler's death is to be found in the poisoning. "Everything beyond this belongs in the sphere of conjecture," was the professor's final word.

Dr. Shkaravski had no use for imaginary "reconstructions of a shooting." "The fact of the poisoning," he told me, "is incontrovertibly established. No matter what is asserted today, our Commission could not detect any traces of a gun shot on May 8, 1945. Hitler poisoned himself."

15

Heinrich Himmler once announced what would be the apotheosis that the rulers of the Third Reich intended to prepare for their Führer: "Right after the war we shall build a house which will be the largest and most magnificent house in the world. We started with plans as early as 1938. It will be built on the Königsplatz in Berlin. The costs for this house are estimated at fifty billion marks. The height of the house will be 355 meters, the diameter 1500 meters. The foundation alone will cost 3 billion marks. It will be a house such as the world has never seen. It will contain ballrooms and halls with room for two to three hundred thousand people. In the cellar we shall build a vault more gigantic and magnificent than the Pharaohs ever dreamed

[6] "Gröfaz"—abbreviation for "grösster Feldherr aller Zeiten," a name given to Hitler by his associates.

of and built. And this will one day be Adolf Hitler's tomb." [1]

This day never came. Instead of it there came the day when the soldier Ivan Churakov pulled the dreadfully disfigured corpse of Adolf Hitler from the rubble in front of the ruins of the Chancellery. That largest house in the world was not built; the German World Empire was doomed to destruction. Wars do not always end as they have been planned by those who have frivolously started them. Adolf Hitler's death is a thought-provoking reminder.

[1] Joachim Besgen, *Der stille Befehl* (Munich, 1960).

Appendix

I. Protocol Concerning the Discovery of the Goebbels Family

DOCUMENT
Identification of the corpses of the German Minister of Propaganda Josef Goebbels, Goebbels' wife, and their 6 children

Berlin, May 3, 1945

We, the undersigned, Administrative Chief, Counter Intelligence SMERSH, 1st Byelorussian Front, Lieutenant General Vadis; Deputy Administrative Chief, Counter Intelligence SMERSH, 1st Byelorussian Front, Major General Melnikov; Section Chief, Counter Intelligence SMERSH, 3rd Shock Army, Colonel Mirozhnichenko; Administrative Section Chief, Counter Intelligence SMERSH, 1st Byelorussian Front, Lieutenant Colonel Barzukov; Section Chief, Counter Intelligence SMERSH, 79th Rifle Corps, Lieutenant Colonel Klimenko; Chief, Political Section, 79th Rifle Corps, Colonel Krylov; Chief, Reconnaissance, 3rd Shock Army, Lieutenant Colonel Gvozd; Section Chief, Counter Intelligence SMERSH, 207th Rifle Division, Major Aksyanov; Deputy Section Chief, Counter Intelligence SMERSH, 207th Rifle Division, Major Khasin; Sub-Section Chief, Counter Intelligence SMERSH, 3rd Shock Army, Major Bystrov; Operations Chief, Counter Intelli-

79

gence Administration SMERSH, 1st Byelorussian Front, Captain Khelimski; Medical Officer, 79th Rifle Corps, Medical Service, Lieutenant Colonel Grachov; Interpreter for German—Chief of Investigating Group, Reconnaissance, 3rd Shock Army, Captain Alperovich, drew up the present Document as follows:

On May 2, 1945, in the center of Berlin, in the bunker of the German Chancellery, Lieutenant Colonel Klimenko and Majors Bystrov and Khasin discovered, in the presence of Berlin citizens —the Germans Lange, Wilhelm, the Chancellery cook, and Schneider, Karl, chief garage mechanic of the Chancellery—a few meters from the entrance door at 17.00 hours the partially charred corpses of a man and a woman; the corpse of the man was smallish, the twisted foot of his right leg (clubfoot) was inside a partially charred metal prosthesis, on the corpse were found the remnants of a charred Party uniform of the NSDAP and a scorched gold Party badge; next to the charred body of the woman a partially scorched gold cigarette case was discovered and on the corpse a gold Party badge of the NSDAP and a scorched gold brooch.

At the head of the two corpses lay two Walther pistols No. 1 (damaged by fire).

On May 3 of the same year the platoon leader of Counter Intelligence Section SMERSH, 207th Rifle Division, Senior Lieutenant Ilyin, found in a separate room in the Chancellery bunker the corpses of children [1] aged three through fourteen, lying on their beds. They were dressed in light nightgowns and exhibited symptoms of poisoning.

The above-mentioned corpses having been recognized as those of Dr. Goebbels, his wife, and their children, all corpses were taken, for post-mortem examination and identification by persons who had known them intimately, to the premises of the Counter Intelligence Section SMERSH, 79th Rifle Corps of the 1st Byelorussian Front.

For identification of the corpses on the premises, the following prisoners of war—the personal representative of Grand Admiral

[1] Five girls and one boy.

Doenitz at Führer Headquarters, Vice-Admiral Voss, Hans Erich, born 1897; chief garage mechanic of the Chancellery, Schneider, Karl Friedrich Wilhelm; and the Chancellery cook, Lange, Wilhelm—were consulted, all of whom knew Goebbels, his wife, and his children well.

Vice-Admiral Voss, Lange, and Schneider identified the corpses unequivocally, during interrogation and in confrontation with the corpses, as Goebbels, his wife and children. Asked on what distinguishing features he based his assertion that these were none other than Goebbels, his wife and children, Vice-Admiral Voss declared that he recognized in the charred male corpse the former Reich Minister of Propaganda Dr. Goebbels by the following distinguishing marks: the partially charred body had an unmistakable likeness to Goebbels, confirmed by the shape of the skull, the lines of the mouth, the brace which Goebbels wore on the right leg, by the presence of the gold Party badge of the NSDAP and the remnants of the charred Party uniform. At the same time Voss confirmed that he had spent the last days (for three weeks) up to May 1 of this year continuously at Führer Headquarters and personally had met Hitler, Goebbels, and their closest entourage. On April 30 of this year Voss learned of Hitler's suicide and of Goebbels' appointment as Chancellor of the Reich.

On May 1 of this year Voss saw Goebbels for the last time at 20.30 hours in the air-raid bunker, where Hitler's Headquarters were housed; at this time Goebbels told Voss that he would follow Hitler's example, i.e., that he would end his life by suicide.

Voss recognized in the partially charred female corpse the wife of Goebbels and explained his certainty by the comment that because of its height (more than medium height) and because of the gold Party badge of the NSDAP *this was the body of Goebbels' wife*. (She was the only German woman wearing this badge; it had been handed to her by Hitler three days before his suicide.)

Further, on examining the cigarette case found near the female body, the inscription in German script "Adolf Hitler—29.X.34"

8 1

was discovered on the inside cover. Voss testified that the case had been used by Goebbels' wife during the last three weeks.

On inspecting the children's bodies Voss identified all of them without exception as Goebbels' children, having seen them all repeatedly; one of the girls, the approximately three-year-old Goebbels daughter Heidi, had visited in Voss's apartment on various occasions.

The above-mentioned persons who had been consulted in the identification of the bodies—the cook Lange and chief garage mechanic Schneider—confirmed emphatically that they both recognized Dr. Goebbels in the partially charred male body, basing their assertion on the shape of the face, the stature of the body, the skull formation, and the metal brace of the right leg.

In the presence of the military personnel enumerated in the present document, the cook Lange also recognized the children's corpses as Goebbels' children; two children he named by their first names, the girl Hilde and the boy Helmut, both of whom he knew personally for some time.

During the external examination of the children's bodies Lieutenant Colonel Grachov, Medical Service, Army Corps, established that the death of the children was caused by introducing the toxic carboxyhemoglobin into the organism.

On the basis of these testimonies we, the undersigned, conclude that the partially charred corpses—of the man, the woman, and the six children—are the corpses of the German Minister of Propaganda Dr. Josef Goebbels, his wife, and their children.

Deposition made in the present Document.

The testimonies of Voss, Lange, and Schneider, who were consulted for identification, were given by them through the interpreter for German, Chief of Investigating Group, Reconnaissance, 3rd Shock Army, Captain Alperovich.

Administrative Chief, Counter Intelligence SMERSH
1st Byelorussian Front
Lieutenant General
signed (A. Vadis)

Deputy Administrative Chief, Counter Intelligence SMERSH
1st Byelorussian Front
Major General
signed   (Melnikov)

Section Chief, Counter Intelligence SMERSH
3rd Shock Army
Colonel
signed   (Mirozhnichenko)

Administrative Section Chief, Counter Intelligence SMERSH
1st Byelorussian Front
Lieutenant Colonel
signed   (Barzukov)

Section Chief, Counter Intelligence SMERSH
79th Rifle Corps
Lieutenant Colonel
signed   (Klimenko)

Chief, Political Section
79th Rifle Corps
Colonel
signed   (Krylov)

Chief, Reconnaissance
3rd Shock Army
Lieutenant Colonel
signed   (Gvozd)

Section Chief, Counter Intelligence SMERSH
207th Rifle Division
Major
signed   (Aksyanov)

Deputy Section Chief, Counter Intelligence SMERSH
207th Rifle Division
Major
signed   (Khasin)

Sub-Section Chief, Counter Intelligence SMERSH
3rd Shock Army
Major
signed (Bystrov)

Operations Chief, Counter Intelligence Administration SMERSH
1st Byelorussian Front
Captain
signed (Khelimski)

Medical Officer
79th Rifle Corps, Medical Service
Lieutenant Colonel
signed (Grachov)

Interpreter for German—Chief of Investigating Group, Reconnaissance
3rd Shock Army
Captain
signed (Alperovich)

The contents of the present Document were orally translated by interpreter Alperovich from Russian into German, understood by us, and confirmed with our signatures:

The persons who confirmed the identity of the corpses on inspection:

German Armed Forces prisoner of war
Vice-Admiral
signed (Voss)

Chancellery Cook
signed (Lange)

Chief Garage Mechanic of the Chancellery
signed (Schneider)

II. Autopsy Reports

DOCUMENT NO. 1
concerning the forensic-medical examination of
the corpse of an unknown girl, appearing to be
approximately 15 years old (a daughter of Goebbels?) [1]

7.V.1945, Berlin-Buch,
Mortuary, Field Hospital for Surgery No. 496

The Commission, consisting of Chief Expert, Forensic Medicine, 1st Byelorussian Front, Medical Service, Lieutenant Colonel Shkaravski F.Y., Chief Anatomical Pathologist, Red Army, Medical Service, Lieutenant Colonel Krayevski N.A., Acting Chief Anatomical Pathologist, 1st Byelorussian Front, Medical Service, Major Marants A.Y., Army Expert, Forensic Medicine, 3rd Shock Army, Medical Service, Major Boguslavski Y.I., and Army Anatomical Pathologist, 3rd Shock Army, Medical Service, Major Gulkevich Y.V., on orders of the member of the Military Council 1st Byelorussian Front, Lieutenant General Telegin, of May 3, 1945, performed the forensic-medical examination of an unknown girl (presumably the corpse of a daughter of Goebbels).

Results of the examination:

A. EXTERNAL EXAMINATION

The corpse is that of a girl appearing to be about 15 years old, well nourished, dressed in a light-blue nightgown trimmed with lace. Height: 1 m 58 cm. Chest measurements on the nipple line —65 cm. Coloration of epidermis and of visible mucous membranes, light pink with bluish tint. On the back, red livor mortis spots with bluish tint which do not disappear on application of pressure. Fingernails bluish. In the region of the shoulder blades and the buttocks, the skin, because of pressure, distinctly pale. Dirty-green discoloration of abdominal skin, due to putrefaction.

[1] Helga Goebbels, age 12.

8 5

Rigor mortis noticeable only in the joints of the feet. Shape of head longish, sloping laterally. Head hair long, dark blond, plaited, shape of face oval, pointed toward the chin. Forehead slightly receding. Color of eyebrows dark blond, long lashes. Color of iris blue. Nose straight, regular, small, eyes closed. Blood content of conjunctiva much increased. Nasal bones and cartilage appear uninjured to palpation. Nostrils and outer auditory canals unobstructed. Mouth closed. Tip of the tongue locked between the teeth. On turning the corpse and pressing the chest cage, excretion of blood serum from mouth and nose of the body and emanation of a faint smell of bitter almonds.

The mouth contains 28 teeth: 8 incisors, 4 canines, 8 bicuspids, 8 molars. The upper and lower jaws have 14 teeth each. No enamel defects. In the mouth, between gums and cheek, the tip of a bluish glass ampule with a small red spot in the center and several glass splinters of the ampule wall were found.

Chest cage normally developed, mammary glands small, no underarm hair noticeable. Abdomen flat. External genital organs normally developed. Labia major and mons Veneris covered with hair to the upper rim of the symphysis. Hymen annular. Bones of the extremities appear uninjured to palpation. Feet in the joints markedly extended. No signs of use of violence on the body surface.

B. INTERNAL EXAMINATION

Thoracic and abdominal organs in their normal positions. The pericardium contains approximately two teaspoonfuls of clear serous fluid. On the posterior and anterior surfaces of both lungs and also between the lobes above the pleura, numerous hemorrhages of varying size, from 1.5 mm. to 3 mm. in diameter, are noted. Both lungs are crimson on the outer surface, dark red on the inner surface, and spongy to the touch. On pressure, the cut surfaces of both lungs excrete small quantities of a foamy dark red liquid. The mucous membrane of the upper respiratory tracts is dark red. The heart is the size of the right fist of the

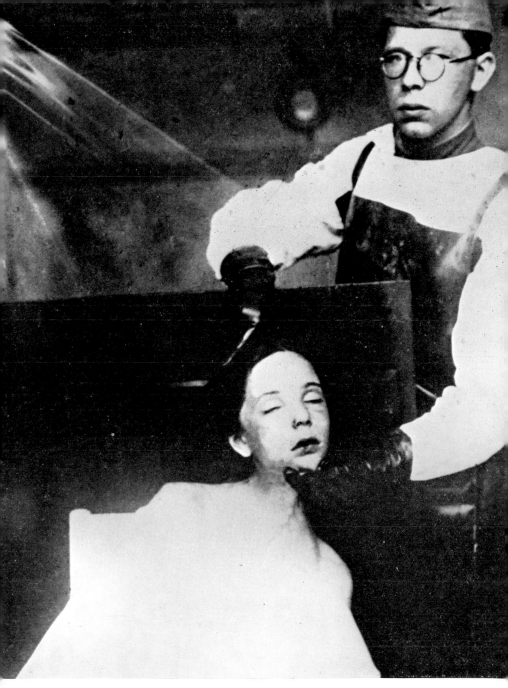

Helga Goebbels after autopsy in Berlin-Buch

Blondi's corpse

corpse. Weight of the heart 200 g., in the cardiac ventricles dark, liquid blood. Heart muscle of flaccid consistence. Thickness of wall of right ventricle 0.3 cm., of left ventricle 0.6 cm. Cardiac valves thin and transparent. Pulmonary artery unobstructed. Lining of aorta smooth and glistening.

Peritoneum smooth and glistening, about 2 tablespoonfuls of free peritoneal fluid present. Mucous membrane lining of the esophagus bluish. Stomach contains approximately 200 cc. of a yellowish, foodlike substance. Pleating of mucous membrane of stomach flattened. Contents of intestines typical. Mucous membrane of small intestine and colon somewhat pale. Liver measurements 22 x 11 x 13 x 9 cm.; liver well supplied with blood, of normal firmness, tracery somewhat effaced. The gall bladder contains about 20 cc. of yellowish bile; its mucous membrane is granulated. Bile duct unobstructed. The pancreas is in the state of post-mortem softening. Measurements of spleen 10 x 5.5 x 2 cm. Spleen capsule wrinkled, the cut surface a dark cherry red, flaccid (onset of putrefaction). Adrenal glands pale and softened. Both kidneys of equal size 9.5 x 5 x 3 cm., their capsules are easily detachable, surface is smooth, pattern on cut surface effaced (putrefaction effect). Mucous membrane of the renal region pale.

Uterus firm, 4 cm. long, at height of Fallopian tubes 3 x 2 cm. wide. External orifice in slit form, closed. In the cavity a small quantity of mucus, interuterine membrane pale. No remarkable changes in the ovaries and Fallopian tubes.

Skull bones intact, vessels of the dura mater somewhat engorged; in the transverse sinus a small quantity of liquid blood. Marked engorgement of meningeal blood vessels. Brain matter exudes a marked smell of bitter almonds. Brain ventricles contain a small quantity of clear fluid. The vascular plexus is well supplied with blood.

Retained for medical-forensic examination:

1) jar—section of stomach with contents.
2) jar—sections of small intestine and colon with contents.
3) jar—sections of lungs, heart, liver, spleen, and kidneys.

4) jar—section of brain.

5) test tube with blood.

The enumerated objects, with no preservative added, were transmitted 7/5 for poison tests to the Medical-Epidemiological Field Laboratory No. 291.

N O T E : Exhibit appended to the document: Test tube with splinters of a glass ampule which were found in the mouth of the body.

Signatures of the Commission:

Chief Expert, Forensic Medicine, 1st Byelorussian Front
Medical Service, Lieutenant Colonel
signed (Shkaravski)

Chief Pathological Anatomist, Red Army
Medical Service, Lieutenant Colonel
signed (Krayevski)

Acting Chief Anatomical Pathologist, 1st Byelorussian Front
Medical Service, Major
signed (Marants)

Army Expert, Forensic Medicine, 3rd Shock Army
Medical Service, Major
signed (Boguslavski)

Army Anatomical Pathologist, 3rd Shock Army
Medical Service, Major
signed (Gulkevich)

CONCLUSION

Based on the forensic-medical autopsy of the corpse of a girl of about 15 and the forensic-chemical test of her internal organs, the Commission reached the following conclusions:

1. The autopsy revealed no injuries or pathological changes which might have caused the death of the dead girl.

2. Splinters of a crushed glass ampule were found in the mouth, upon opening of the corpse a marked bitter almond smell was perceived, and the chemical examination of the internal organs established the presence of cyanide compounds.

The conclusion reached is therefore that the death of the 15-year-old girl was caused by poisoning with a cyanide compound.

Signatures of the Commission:

Same as on p. 88.

DOCUMENT NO. 3
concerning the forensic-medical examination of the corpse of a German shepherd dog

> *7.V.1945, Berlin-Buch,*
> *Mortuary, Field Hospital for Surgery No. 496*

The Commission, consisting of Chief Expert, Forensic Medicine, 1st Byelorussian Front, Medical Service, Lieutenant Colonel Shkaravski F.Y., Chief Anatomical Pathologist, Red Army, Medical Service, Lieutenant Colonel Krayevski N.A., Acting Chief Anatomical Pathologist, 1st Byelorussian Front, Medical Service, Major Marants A.Y., Army Expert, Forensic Medicine, 3rd Shock Army, Medical Service, Major Boguslavski Y.I. and Army Anatomical Pathologist, 3rd Shock Army, Medical Service, Major Gulkevich Y.V., on orders of the member of the 1st Byelorussian Front Military Council, Lieutenant General Telegin, performed the forensic-medical examination of the corpse of the shepherd dog.

Results of the examination:

A. EXTERNAL EXAMINATION

Corpse of the large dog (bitch). Breed: German Shepherd. Color of coat—back dark gray, underbelly light gray. Black markings around muzzle. Tail moderately bushy. Length of the

89

corpse from occipital protuberance to tail joint 91 cm. Teeth white, points of canine teeth somewhat worn.

Teats grayish, well developed, no excretion on pressure.

On the mucous membrane of the tongue, two splinters of a thin-walled glass ampule were found: part of the bottom of the ampule and part of the wall. Minor scratches with smooth edges on the mucous membrane of the palate, mucus inside muzzle bloody. Hemorrhages around the scratches.

No other injuries were noted on the dog's corpse; the longitudinal bones felt intact to palpation.

<h3 style="text-align:center">B. INTERNAL EXAMINATION</h3>

Position of internal organs normal, blood supply moderate. In cardiac and large blood vessels free red blood clots.

Upon opening, a pronounced smell of bitter almond was perceived.

Stomach and intestinal tract contain considerable quantities of half-digested food with unpleasant sour smell.

On examining the internal organs, no pathological changes were noted.

For chemical testing, 10 cc. blood was drawn and put into a test tube; sections of the lungs, the heart, the liver, the kidneys, the spleen, the stomach, and the intestines were put into a glass jar.

The enumerated objects, with no preservatives added, were transmitted to the Medical-Epidemiological Field Laboratory No. 291 for the purpose of forensic-chemical testing for the presence of cyanide compounds and basic poisons.

Signatures of the Commission:

Same as on p. 88.

<h3 style="text-align:center">CONCLUSION</h3>

Based on the forensic-medical examination of the corpse of the German shepherd and the forensic-chemical examination of its

Children	Symptoms	Chemical Analysis	Conclusion
Document No. 1 *Helga* (see pp. 85 ff.)	Splinters of ampule in mouth. Brain matter smells of bitter almond. Color of lungs: red.	Cyanides present	Cyanide poisoning
Document No. 2 *Heide*	Splinters of ampule behind cheek. Brain matter smells of bitter almond.	Cyanides present	Cyanide poisoning
Document No. 8 *Hedda*	Splinters of ampule in mouth. Dissection of tongue yields bitter almond smell.	Cyanides present	Cyanide poisoning
Document No. 9 *Holde*	Splinters of ampule in mouth. Brain and lungs smell of bitter almonds.	Cyanides present	Cyanide poisoning
Document No. 10 *Helmut* (see pp. 107 ff.)	Ampule splinters. Brain and lungs smell of bitter almonds.	Cyanides present	Cyanide poisoning
Document No. 11 *Hilde*	Ampule splinters. Brain and lungs smell of bitter almonds.	Cyanides present	Cyanide poisoning

Documents Nos. 2, 8, 9, and 11 are not reproduced in this book.

internal organs, the Commission reaches the following conclusions:

1. Dissection revealed no injuries or pathological changes which might have caused the death of the dog.

2. In the mucous membrane of the muzzle and of the tongue, splinters of a thin-walled ampule were found, dissection of the cadaver released the smell of bitter almonds, and at the forensic-chemical testing the presence of cyanide compounds was ascertained in the internal organs.

3. We therefore conclude that the death of the dog was caused by poisoning with cyanide compounds.

Signatures of the Commission:

Same as on p. 88.

DOCUMENT NO. 4
concerning the forensic-medical examination of the corpse of a small black dog

> *7.V.1945, Berlin-Buch,*
> *Mortuary, Field Hospital for Surgery No. 496*

The Commission, consisting of Chief Expert, Forensic Medicine, 1st Byelorussian Front, Medical Service, Lieutenant Colonel Shkaravski F.Y., Chief Anatomical Pathologist, Red Army, Medical Service, Lieutenant Colonel Krayevski N.A., Acting Chief Anatomical Pathologist, 1st Byelorussian Front, Medical Service, Major Marants A.Y., Army Expert, Forensic Medicine, 3rd Shock Army, Medical Service, Major Boguslavski Y.I., and Army Anatomical Pathologist, 3rd Shock Army, Medical Service, Major Gulkevich Y.V., on orders of the member of the Military Council, 1st Byelorussian Front, Lieutenant General Telegin, performed the forensic-medical examination and autopsy of the corpse of a small black dog.

Results of the examination:

The corpse is that of a small black dog (bitch) with long, shaggy hair and short tail. Length of the dog from occipital protuberance to joint of tail, 58 cm. Height measurement from the shoulder (upper angle of the shoulder blade) to the tips of the claws 28.5 cm.

The muzzle is filled with red blood clots. The head exhibits a circular shot wound of 1 cm. diameter (bullet entry) above the left ear; wound of exit is located in the lower part of the muzzle between the lower jawbone fork; its measurements are 1.2 cm. x 1.5 cm.; the wound of exit is ragged (perforating shot).

The bullet pathway connecting the two apertures runs through the skull, forming an open fracture in the left half of the lower jaw, in the direction of the oral cavity. The injury is surrounded by hemorrhages. No foreign objects were found in the muzzle. In the abdomen, to the left and right of the rib cage, two 1 cm. diameter apertures caused by a bullet are noted.

B . INTERNAL EXAMINATION

The bullet pathway runs through the abdominal cavity, producing a stellate tear in the liver. The abdominal cavity contains close to 400 cc. liquid blood. During dissection, the typically unpleasant dog smell was perceivable.

Position of internal organs normal, no visible structural changes. Blood quantity reduced, color of blood pink.

For the forensic-chemical test, sections of the liver, the heart, the kidneys, the spleen, the lungs, the stomach, and the intestines were taken and placed in a jar. The organs have been transmitted, with no preservatives added, to the Medical-Epidemiological Field Laboratory for the purpose of chemical testing for the presence of cyanide compounds and basic poisons.

Signatures of the Commission:

Same as on p. 88.

Based on the forensic-medical examination and the autopsy of the cadaver of a small black dog and the forensic-chemical test of its internal organs and blood, the Commission reaches the following conclusions:

1. The examination established a perforating shot through the dog's head while the animal was alive, wound of entrance above the left ear, and a perforating shot through the abdomen. The injuries are by their nature lethal.

2. The forensic-chemical test established the presence of cyanide compounds in the internal organs.

The causes of death are poisoning by cyanide compounds and a lethal head injury with extensive destruction of brain matter.

The method of killing of the dog can be envisaged as follows: First it was probably poisoned by a small dosis of cyanide, and subsequently the poisoned, agonizing dog was shot.

Signatures of the Commission:

Same as on p. 88.

DOCUMENT NO. 5
concerning the forensic-medical examination of
the partially burned corpse of an unknown man
(presumably the corpse of Goebbe')

> *9.V.1945, Berlin-Buch,*
> *Field Hospital for Surgery No. 496*

The Commission, consisting of Chief Expert, Forensic Medicine, 1st Byelorussian Front, Medical Service, Lieutenant Colonel Shkaravski F.Y., Chief Anatomical Pathologist, Red Army, Medical Service, Lieutenant Colonel Krayevski N.A., Acting Chief Anatomical Pathologist, 1st Byelorussian Front, Medical Service, Major Marants A.Y., Army Expert, Forensic Medicine, 3rd Shock Army, Medical Service, Major Boguslavski Y.I., and

Army Anatomical Pathologist, 3rd Shock Army, Medical Service, Major Gulkevich Y.V., on orders of the member of the Military Council, 1st Byelorussian Front, Lieutenant General Telegin, performed the forensic-medical examination of the partially burned corpse of an unknown man.

Results of the examination:

A. EXTERNAL EXAMINATION

Together with the corpse, two singed black leather laced boots were found, the back part of the right boot somewhat wider in comparison with the left. Its width corresponds to the measurements of a leather prosthesis which was delivered together with the corpse. The 2 cm. wide metal brace is intended for the leg and has two annular buckles of the same metal fastening around the leg muscles. The lower part of the brace consists of leather with a metal sole and fits the right foot of the dead man. Under the corpse, burned parts of clothing and a fire-blackened Walther pistol No. 1 were found. Further finds next to the corpse: a piece of singed black wool with a glossy black stripe as it is used in the form of narrow black piping on the outer seam of civilian trousers, the singed braids and part of the collar of the bright yellow NSDAP uniform with yellow-gold silk lining, singed pieces of a white undershirt with the factory markings—4326, 3716, 38 1235, A.S.—11797 APDT, and a shirt front with red, hand-stitched laundry marking "4327-8."

Partially burned dark silk socks stick to the feet of the corpse, around the neck lies a yellow silk tie with a round metal badge bearing the swastika and the lettering NSDAP.

The corpse is that of a man of subnormal stature, appearing to be between 45 and 50 years of age, severely charred, which has taken on the posture of a boxer, with arms extended and half bent in the elbow joints, legs equally half bent in the knee joints, face and neck charred (upper neck portion charred more considerably on the right); they are black. The ear lobes are preserved as shapeless, charred, small protuberances.

95

Contours of skull and face have kept their shape; eyes are closed, somewhat sunken; the nose is moderately large with a small hump in the middle part of the bridge, its width proportionate to its length; mouth half open, the upper teeth large and protruding markedly over the lower ones (prognathism). The forehead is noticeably receding, the face tapers off to the pointed chin.

Skull circumference on the line of the occipital protuberance and the supra-orbital ridge 50 cm. Longest diagonal dimension from occipital protuberance to chin: 24 cm. Maximum dimension across the head: 15 cm.

Laterally the skull is considerably flattened (approaching dolichocephalic). Head hair missing, burned. Mouth half open, lips dry, black, and charred.

Lower half of right arm missing, ends of preserved stump charred, black, crumbling. Left arm and left leg are preserved, scorched, show various deep fissures in the skin tissue and the scorched dehydrated muscles.

Also scorched are the thoracic wall and the left half of the loins. Right thigh and part of right leg charred.

External genital organs have kept their contour but are greatly reduced in size, shrunken, dry.

The skin of the two legs is of parchmentlike consistence, coloration brown. The right leg measures 33.5 cm. from the outer protuberance of the ankle to the upper edge of the outer part of the epiphysis of the shinbone; the left leg measures 38 cm. between the same points. Circumference of the right leg at its thickest is 18 cm., of the left, however, 27 cm.

Although the right leg is charred, the pronounced atrophy compared to the left one can be readily established. Circumference of the thigh around the middle: 35 cm.; of the left, however, 43.5 cm.

The right foot has not been altered by the action of fire. Its sole is twisted inward to such a degree that it stands virtually at a right angle to the leg bone.

Around the joint of the foot there is substantial deformation, foot is shortened and thickened. The left foot measures 21.5 cm., the right, however, (maximal length) 18 cm. The orthopedic appliance accompanying the corpse and described above corresponds exactly to the deformation of the right foot.

Oral Cavity: To preserve the face, a cosmetic incision was made under the left lower jawbone in order to permit a detailed examination of the oral cavity, especially of the left side.

Findings: In comparison to the outer and especially the mandibular incisors, the maxillary inner incisors are large. The first right maxillary incisor overlaps somewhat the second right incisor. The second maxillary bicuspid on the left has a gold filling. The first and second maxillary left molars each have an amalgam filling.

The outer and inner surfaces of the other teeth of the left lower jaw as well as the teeth of the upper jaw exhibit no significant features.

The second bicuspid and the first molar below are about 5 mm. apart. Between the teeth of the right lower jaw a splinter of thin colorless glass, belonging to an ampule, was found.

B. INTERNAL EXAMINATION

Skeletal muscles and those of the internal organs appear boiled and are of a pale grayish red. Position of the internal organs in the thoracic and abdominal cavities normal. All organs are of firm consistence, with the exception of the lungs; the left lung, in particular, is only moderately supplied with blood and somewhat spongy.

Dissection of the lungs released a faint smell of bitter almonds. The pleural cavities contained no fluid, the lungs are unobstructed, the coloration of the cut surface is dark red.

The heart contains some liquid dark blood. Peritoneum smooth, liver firm, dry, of grayish brown coloration, normal contour, shrunken. Spleen small, capsule wrinkled, pattern of kidneys intact. The vermiform appendix measuring 5 cm. is unobstructed, the stomach empty, the mucous membrane shows

97

marked pleating. Bladder empty. Intestines contain a small quantity of typical matter.

The following were taken for chemical testing:

a) 10 cc. blood in a test tube.

b) Sections of the lungs, the heart, the liver, the kidneys, and the spleen were placed in a glass jar.

c) Sections of the stomach and intestines with contents were placed in a second jar.

CONCLUSION

Based on the external examination and the autopsy of the partially burned corpse of an unknown man and the findings of the forensic-chemical examination of his internal organs, the Commission reaches the following conclusions:

1. *Anatomical characteristics of the corpse:*
The corpse of the unknown man is heavily scorched, so that some of its distinguishing features are effaced. For the identification of the person the following is to be taken into consideration:

a) Stature—smaller than average;

b) Age between 45 and 50 years;

c) In consequence of the shortened leg bone and the foot twisted around the joint, the right leg is atrophied and shortened; this explains the presence of an orthopedic appliance for the right foot and of the orthopedic right shoe;

d) Characteristics of the head: laterally flattened, forehead markedly receding, face pronouncedly pointed toward the chin, moderately large nose with small hump;

e) Of particular importance for identification are the state of the teeth of the upper and lower jaws and the considerable number of fillings.

2. *Cause of death:*
The partially burned corpse exhibits no visible signs of severe, lethal injuries or disease.

Upon dissection of the corpse, the smell of bitter almonds was noticed; splinters of an ampule were found in the mouth. Chemical test of the internal organs and of the blood evidenced the presence of cyanide compounds. The conclusion must be drawn that the death of the unknown man was caused by poisoning by a cyanide compound.

Signatures of the Commission:

Same as on p. 88.

DOCUMENT NO. 6
concerning the forensic-medical examination of
the partially burned corpse of an unknown woman
(presumably the wife of Goebbels)

> 9.V.1945, Berlin-Buch,
> Mortuary, Field Hospital for Surgery No. 496

The Commission, consisting of Chief Expert, Forensic Medicine, 1st Byelorussian Front, Medical Service, Lieutenant Colonel Shkaravski F.Y., Chief Anatomical Pathologist, Red Army, Medical Service, Lieutenant Colonel Krayevski N.A., Acting Chief Anatomical Pathologist, Forensic Medicine, 3rd Shock Army, Medical Service, Major Marants A.Y., Army Expert, Forensic Medicine, 3rd Shock Army, Medical Service, Major Boguslavski Y.I., and Army Anatomical Pathologist, 3rd Shock Army, Medical Service, Major Gulkevich Y.V., on orders of the member of the 1st Byelorussian Front Military Council, Lieutenant General Telegin, performed the forensic-medical examination of the partially burned corpse of an unknown woman (presumably the wife of Goebbels).

Results of the examination:

A. EXTERNAL EXAMINATION

Together with the corpse, the charred remains of the clothing were deposited at the mortuary, among them a charred piece of yellowish coffee-brown jersey. Also found in the ashes were fire-blackened metal hair clips, a snap fastener, a buckle, and a round metal badge (copper) with a swastika.

The corpse is that of a woman apparently 30 to 40 years old. Stature (approximate, because of charring) 1 m 56 cm., chest circumference on the nipple line 66 cm. The examination of the charred corpse revealed no signs of malformation or significant abnormalities. Nutritional state: average. The corpse is severely scorched, virtually black throughout. Brown skin of parchmentlike consistence preserved only on certain parts of the dorsum, the buttocks, the right shoulder, the thighs, and one leg. The margins of the skin of the enumerated parts are blackened; there are deep fissures in the skin tissues reaching to the deeply imbedded muscles. Other regions of the body surface are charred in varying degree; the left parietal skull bones and those of the temporal region, as well as the ribs on the right side, are singed. In the gaping cranium dry brain tissue is visible. On the occiput and on part of the right temporal region reddish blond hair of a maximal length of 40 cm. is preserved. In the same region a hairpiece of similar reddish blond hair was found. The hair contained many hair clips as well as ordinary metal hairpins. The face is charred, but its contour is preserved. Nose, lips, cheeks are singed.

Splinters from a thin-walled ampule with a blue tip were found in the mouth. The partially burned jawbones lie detached in the oral cavity and could be readily extracted.

The upper jaw has 14 teeth, of which 4 are natural incisors and 2 canine teeth. The second bicuspid left is artificial, on a gold support with a bridge anchored on the first bicuspid.

The first left molar has a small filling, the second left molar has a gold half crown and a filling, the first right bicuspid has an amalgam filling, the first right molar has a gold filling and the second molar two gold fillings.

Lower jaw—the front part of the mandibula is completely preserved, the right vertical section is also preserved, the left one missing. In the lower jaw are 4 natural incisors, 2 canine

100

teeth, and the first 2 bicuspids; these teeth are white, the masticating surfaces moderately worn. The second bicuspid to the left is half-capped in gold, the left molar is fitted with a large filling.

The first bicuspid on the right is heavily worn, the second bicuspid is missing.

The first right molar is missing; a thin gold platelet merging into a gold bridge and crown over the second and third right molars is anchored there.

Chest cage cylinder-shaped, mammary glands small, somewhat charred. As a result of the burning, there is a large defect in the right armpit region. Stomach flat, external genital organs charred.

B. INTERNAL EXAMINATION

Positions of thoracic organs normal, lungs unobstructed. The right lung considerably shrunken, firm, singed. The left lung spongy, color pink-gray (appears boiled). Tracheae and bronchiae shrunken from action of fire, their mucous membrane pale pink. The shrunken heart kept its contour, the muscles appear boiled, in the heart chambers and in the large cardiac vessels thick red blood is noted.

The abdominal organs are normally positioned. Peritoneum and organs are dry and appear boiled. The liver is firm, boiled. Spleen capsule wrinkled, cut surface red. Pattern of the kidneys preserved. Stomach empty, marked pleating of mucous membrane. The intestines contain a small quantity of typical matter, vermiform appendix preserved. Bladder compressed, empty. Uterus normal, pear-shaped. Measurements: 7 x 4 x 3 cm. Interuterine cavity unobstructed. All organs smell of burning.

The following were taken for chemical testing:

1. 10 cc. blood (in a test tube).

2. Sections of the lungs, liver, spleen, kidneys, stomach, and intestines; everything put into one jar.

The objects enumerated above were transmitted, with no

preservatives added, to the Medical-Epidemiological Field Laboratory No. 291 for forensic-chemical testing for the presence of cyanide compounds and basic poisons.

Appended to the Document:

1. Test tube with splinter of glass from the thin-walled ampule with light blue tip which was taken from the oral cavity of the body.
2. A Walther pistol No. 1.
3. A piece of burned shirt.
4. Charred hair clips, a snap fastener, and other items.
5. Lower jaw with 12 teeth, among them 3 with gold crowns.
6. Upper jaw with 14 teeth.
7. Nazi badge.
8. A strand of reddish blond hair.
9. Part of a reddish blond hairpiece.

Signatures of the Commission:

Same as on p. 88.

Same as on p. 88.

CONCLUSION

Based on the forensic-medical examination and autopsy of the corpse of an unknown woman and the findings of the forensic-medical examination of her organs, the Commission reached the following conclusions:

1. *Anatomical characteristics of the body:*
As a result of the extensive burning of the body, the external features of the dead woman cannot be described, but the following has been established:

    a) Stature about 156 cm. (one hundred fifty-six cm.).

    b) Age between 30 and 40 years.

    c) Color of hair: reddish blond. Maximal length of available hair: up to 40 cm. The dead woman wore a hairpiece of the same color.

d) Nutritional state of the body: average.

e) The most significant anatomical find for use in identification of the person are the upper and lower jaws with a great number of artificial teeth, crowns, and fillings (see autopsy report).

2. *Cause of death:*

The charred corpse exhibited no visible evidence of severe, lethal injuries or disease.

The forensic-chemical test of the internal organs established the presence of cyanide compounds.

At the autopsy, splinters of a thin-walled glass ampule with light blue tip were found in the mouth.

The conclusion reached must therefore be that the death of the unknown woman was caused by poisoning with a cyanide compound.

Signatures of the Commission:

Same as on p. 88.

DOCUMENT NO. 7

*concerning the forensic-medical examination of
the corpse of the Chief of the German General
Staff, Major General Krips* [1]

> 9.V.1945, Berlin-Buch,
> *Mortuary, Field Hospital for Surgery No. 496*

The Commission, consisting of Chief Expert, Forensic Medicine, 1st Byelorussian Front, Medical Service, Lieutenant Colonel Shkaravski F.Y., Chief Anatomical Pathologist, Red Army, Medical Service, Lieutenant Colonel Krayevski N.A., Acting Chief Anatomical Pathologist, Forensic Medicine, 3rd Shock Army, Medical Service, Major Marants A.Y., Army

[1] This should be General Krebs.

Expert, Forensic Medicine, 3rd Shock Army, Medical Service, Major Boguslavski Y.I., and Army Anatomical Pathologist, 3rd Shock Army, Medical Service, Major Gulkevich Y.V., on orders of the member of the 1st Byelorussian Front Military Council, Lieutenant General Telegin, performed the forensic-medical examination of the corpse of Major General of the German Armed Forces, Krips.

Results of the examination:

A. EXTERNAL EXAMINATION

Clothing of the corpse:

1. Gray-green German tunic with remnants of torn-off epaulettes and red collar facing edged with gold braid.

Above the right upper breast pocket a gold-embroidered insignia with swastika.

On the same pocket, left, is fastened a die-cast Nazi badge with the date 1939. On the left pocket an insignia of black metal—an embossed German soldier's helmet with swastika, beneath the helmet two crossed swords, in the second buttonhole left of the tunic a red ribbon with one black and two light narrow vertical stripes. The tunic is unbuttoned.

2. Gray riding breeches with leather pipings, belt buttons unfastened.

3. Feet clothed in dark gray socks.

4. Turquoise-colored tight-meshed collarless jersey undershirt, with 3 fastened buttons.

5. White underpants.

6. Clothing complete and clean.

The corpse is that of a man appearing to be 45 to 50 years old. Stature 1 m 75 cm., of normal, athletic build; nutritional state, above average.

Color of epidermis glowing red with bluish tint. Livor mortis spots of the same coloration, color intensity remains unchanged on pressure. Rigor mortis persistent in all muscle groups.

Head shaved, shape of face oval. Ear and nasal passages

unobstructed. Nasal bones and cartilage appear uninjured to palpation. Eyes closed, cornea opaque. Visible mucous membranes of eyelids, nose, and lips bluish red. Mouth half open, teeth appear healthy, white, considerably worn. Two gold crowns with bridge on the bicuspids, in the lower jaw right and left. In the upper jaw visible gold filling in the first bicuspid right and in two bicuspids left.

No glass splinters found in the oral cavity.

Chest cage cylinder-shaped, on the front surface thick coat of hair, dark mixed with gray. Abdomen moderately bloated, normally developed external genital organs.

Injuries noted on the corpse:

1. On the neck to the right, 1.5 cm. from the right jaw angle, a 1 x 1.3 cm. wide lacerated wound, with irregularly torn edges, depth of wound ¾ cm., wound surrounded by hematoma.

2. In the right cheekbone region, 2.5 cm. from the auditory canal, a vertical wound measuring 4 cm. in length and 0.5 cm. in width. Ragged, irregular edges, cross-striped tissue and connective tissue visible. Depth of wound: 0.75 cm., hemorrhage into the tissues around wound margins.

3. In the left temporal region, a lacerated surface wound with ragged edges. Subcutaneous hemorrhage into the surrounding tissues.

4. In the region of the right orbital ridge a subcutaneous hemorrhage measuring 4 x 3 cm.

No other injuries were noted; the longitudinal bones of the corpse are intact.

B. INTERNAL EXAMINATION

Bones of the skull uninjured. Upon opening of the brain, marked bitter almond smell perceivable. Meninges without noticeable changes, brain vessels somewhat dilated. In the ventricles a reduced quantity of clear, yellow fluid.

Structure of brain matter typical; gray layer easily distinguishable from white layer.

Positions of thoracic and abdominal organs normal. Upon their opening, marked smell of bitter almonds.

The lungs are unobstructed, pleura in the pleural cavities dark red. The lungs are spongy, well supplied with blood. Bronchiae unobstructed, mucous membrane reddish.

The heart is the size of the dead man's fist. Weight: 390 g. Heart muscle of normal firmness, reddish gray. Cardiac valves thin, glistening. The heart contains a considerable quantity of liquid red blood.

Peritoneum thin, glistening, no free peritoneal fluid present. Weight of liver: 1700 g., liver has tapered front edge, pattern somewhat effaced, blood supply moderate.

Weight of spleen: 300 g., capsule wrinkled, spleen matter dirty red, altered by putrefaction.

Weight of each kidney: 190 g., fibrous kidney capsule easily detachable, tracery somewhat effaced, signs of putrefaction. Bladder contains close to 100 cc. of yellow, clear urine.

Stomach collapsed, empty, its mucous membrane pinkish gray. Intestines not bloated, empty, mucous membrane pinkish gray.

For chemical testing, the following were taken:

1. 10 cc. blood, in test tube.

2. Sections of brain, lungs, heart, liver, kidneys, spleen, stomach, and intestines, in one jar.

The listed objects were transmitted, with no preservative added, via Section SMERSH of the 3rd Shock Army to the Medical-Epidemiological Field Laboratory No. 291 for chemical analysis for cyanide compounds and basic poisons.

Signature of the Commission:

Same as on p. 88.

CONCLUSION

Based on the external examination and the autopsy of the corpse of the Chief of the German General Staff, Major General KREBS, and the forensic-chemical tests of his internal organs, the Commission reaches the following conclusion:

1. The three head wounds found on the corpse are in the nature of lacerated wounds and belong to the group of minor injuries. They probably originated when the body of the dead man, in his death agony, fell and struck some protruding, sharp-cornered object.

2. The forensic-medical test of the internal organs of the dead man established the presence of cyanide compounds.

3. The death of General KREBS was therefore obviously caused by poisoning with cyanide compounds.

Signatures of the Commission:

Same as on p. 88.

DOCUMENT NO. 10
concerning the forensic-medical examination of the corpse of a boy appearing to be about 12 years of age (son of Goebbels) [1]

> 8.V.1945, Berlin-Buch,
> Mortuary, Field Hospital for Surgery No. 496

The Commission, consisting of Chief Expert, Forensic Medicine, 1st Byelorussian Front, Medical Service, Lieutenant Colonel Shkaravski F.Y., Chief Anatomical Pathologist, Red Army, Medical Service, Lieutenant Colonel Krayevski N.A., Acting Chief Anatomical Pathologist, Forensic Medicine, 3rd Shock Army, Medical Service, Major Marants A.Y., Army Expert, Forensic Medicine, 3rd Shock Army, Medical Service, Major Boguslavski Y.I., and Army Anatomical Pathologist, 3rd Shock Army, Medical Service, Major Gulkevich Y.V., on orders of the member of the 1st Byelorussian Front Military Council, Lieutenant General Telegin, of May 3, 1945, performed the forensic-medical examination of the corpse of a boy

[1] Helmut Goebbels, age 9.

appearing to be about 12 years of age, presumably the son of Goebbels.

Results of the examination:

The corpse is that of a boy appearing to be about 12 years of age; it is clad in pajamas of white material with small green-blue and red flower pattern, clothing clean. Height 136 cm., chest circumference 56 cm., skull circumference on the line of the occipital protuberance and the supra-orbital ridge 55 cm., build normal, well nourished. The head is laterally somewhat flattened, covered with dark blond hair of a maximal length of 20 cm. Face longish, particularly toward the chin. Shape of nose regular, well proportioned. Eyes closed. Color of iris bluish-gray.

The mouth contains 28 teeth, 14 in each jawbone. Teeth white, healthy. The upper front teeth somewhat protuberant over the lower ones, on the outer surface of the upper teeth a wire prosthesis intended to correct the protrusion of the teeth by an arch attached to the back molars.

In the mouth, several small splinters of a thin-walled glass ampule were found. Small scratches on the tongue and on the mucous membrane of the gums were noted. The oral mucus is blood-colored.

Chest cage cylinder-shaped. Abdomen flat. External genital organs normally developed, no hair covering on the mons Veneris and the armpits. No abnormalities in the extremities noted.

Color of epidermis and visible mucous membranes pink. The posterior and lateral body surfaces exhibit reddish livor mortis spots, not disappearing on pressure. Minimal rigor mortis, subsisting only in the lower extremities. Aside from the above-mentioned scratches in the mouth, no injuries were found on the body. The longitudinal bones felt intact to palpation.

Cranium unremarkable, skull bones intact. Meninges and brain tissue somewhat tense. Vessels of the soft meninges dilated. In the brain ventricles a small quantity of a straw-colored fluid. Structure of brain tissue typical, gray matter well separated from white matter. Upon opening of the brain marked smell of bitter almonds.

Positions of thoracic and abdominal organs normal. Serous membranes thin, glistening, pink-colored. The serous cavities contain a moderate quantity of straw-colored, clear fluid. Lungs free—spongy; cut surface red; under pressure, the section exudes ample liquid blood. Respiratory tracts unobstructed, mucous membranes pale pink. Upon opening of the lungs a marked smell of bitter almonds. The heart is the size of the fist of the dead boy, its weight 130 g. Heart muscles are flesh-colored, fairly firm. Cardiac valves thin, transparent; the heart contains liquid red blood.

The liver weighs 800 g., its edge is tapered, firmness normal, tracery clear, blood supply ample.

The spleen weighs 95 g., surface wrinkled, color of cut surface pale red. Weight of each kidney 75 g., capsule easily detachable, pattern somewhat effaced.

Stomach empty, mucous membrane a dirty red; intestines bloated, contents typical, mucous membrane pleated, of dirty coloration. Bladder contains 10 cc. clear urine.

Appended a test tube with splinters of a glass ampule which were found in the oral cavity.

N O T E : The following were retained for testing:
1. Test tube with cardiac blood.
2. Glass jar with sections of lungs, liver, heart, kidneys, and spleen.
3. Glass jar with part of stomach, including contents.
4. Glass jar with sections of small intestine and colon, including contents.
5. Glass jar with part of brain.

All the enumerated objects have been transmitted via Section SMERSH of the 3rd Shock Army to the Medical-Epidemiological Field Laboratory No. 292 for forensic-medical testing for the presence of cyanide compounds and basic poisons.

Signatures of the Commission:

Same as on p. 88.

CONCLUSION

Based on the forensic-medical examination of the corpse of the boy and the forensic-chemical test of his internal organs, the Commission reaches the following conclusions:

1. The autopsy revealed no injuries or pathological changes which might have caused the death of the boy.

2. Fragments of a crushed glass ampule were found in the mouth, during dissection a marked bitter almond smell was perceivable, and the chemical test of the internal organs established the presence of cyanide compounds.

It must be concluded that the death of the approximately 12-year-old boy was caused by poisoning with cyanide compounds.

Signatures of the Commission:

Same as on p. 88.

DOCUMENT NO. 13
concerning the forensic-medical examination of
the partially burned corpse of an unknown woman
(presumably the wife of Hitler)

> 8.V.1945, Berlin-Buch,
> Mortuary, Field Hospital for Surgery No. 496

The Commission, consisting of Chief Expert, Forensic Medicine, 1st Byelorussian Front, Medical Service, Lieutenant Colonel Shkaravski F.Y., Chief Anatomical Pathologist, Red

Army, Medical Service, Lieutenant Colonel Krayevski N.A., Acting Chief Anatomical Pathologist, 1st Byelorussian Front, Medical Service, Major Marants A.Y., Army Expert, Forensic Medicine, 3rd Shock Army, Medical Service, Major Boguslavski Y.I., and Army Anatomical Pathologist, 3rd Shock Army, Medical Service, Major Gulkevich Y.V., on orders of the member of the 1st Byelorussian Front Military Council, Lieutenant General Telegin, of May 3, 1945, performed the forensic-medical examination of the corpse of a woman (presumably Hitler's wife).

Results of the examination:

A. EXTERNAL EXAMINATION

The corpse is that of a woman, stature ca. 150 cm. (measurements are approximate, since several parts of the body are charred and severely disfigured). Age difficult to gauge, presumably between 30 and 40 years. Almost the entire top of the cranium and the upper part of the frontal cranium are missing; they are burned. Only fragments of the burned and broken occipital and temporal bones are preserved, as is the lower part of the left facial bones. Nose charred, mouth half open. Tongue black, dry, charred.

Upper jaw: charred, alveolar processes missing; between the palate and the tongue a molar and the prong of a tooth with broad socket are exposed on the right. In the upper left there are a loose canine and 2 molars. The other teeth in the upper jaw are missing. In the mouth, a piece of yellow metal (gold) of irregular shape measuring 6 x 3 mm. was found (presumably a filling).

On the left side of the lower jaw the second incisor with a dark point, the canine tooth, 2 bicuspids, and 2 molars are preserved. All of them are moderately worn, and show visible changes due to dental caries. On the right side no teeth were found, probably because of burning. In the oral cavity a bridge of yellow metal (gold) was found under the tongue, unattached,

111

which connects the second right bicuspid and the third right molar by means of a gold crown; on the metal plate of the bridge the first and second artificial white molars are attached in front; their appearance is almost undistinguishable from natural teeth.

In the oral cavity, large yellowish glass splinters measuring 1-5 square millimeters of a thin-walled ampule were found under the tongue and between the teeth.

The soft tissues of the neck are charred. Mammary glands small, dry, cut surface yellow. Right part of thorax and abdomen severely burned; a large part of the tissue is missing here, the ensuing openings in the thoracic and abdominal cavities exposing the internal organs to view. Sections of the skin tissue were preserved in the region of the left shoulder blade, the loins, and the left buttock. The lower third of the right upper arm bone is burned, soft tissue dry, black, charred fragments of the bones of the right lower arm preserved, right hand greatly disfigured (by fire).

Lower extremities black because of charring, dry, deformed. In skin tissues and muscles many deep fissures. No signs of fractures. Both feet are in somewhat better state of preservation, their skin coloration a dirty brown.

Injuries to the body: In the region of the left frontal part of the thorax on the parasternal line in the second intercostal space, there is an aperture of irregular shape measuring 1 x 0.9 cm., surrounded by clearly distinguishable hemorrhages; another similar aperture is found further to the right in a charred region.

B. INTERNAL EXAMINATION

Between the muscles of the second intercostal space close to the chest bone two apertures which extend into the thoracic cavity. In the left pleural cavity liquid blood in quantity of nearly 500 cc. was noted. Right lung is shrunken, of liverlike consistence, left lung spongy, dark red. In the upper lobe of the left lung two large perforating injuries measuring 0.4 x 0.6 cm.

112

have been noted. In the left pleural cavity six metal fragments (steel) measuring up to 0.5 sq. cm. were found. In the upper frontal part of the pericardium two apertures measuring 0.8 x 0.4 cm. are visible. They are surrounded by a clearly discernible hemorrhage; similar injuries are present in the direction of the left pleural cavity.

The pericardium contains close to 3 cc. of blood. Heart muscle boiled, grayish red. Valves thin, glistening. In the cardiac chambers a small quantity of dark, liquid blood. Pulmonary artery unobstructed. Lining of the aorta smooth and glistening. Position of the abdominal organs normal. Organs dry, shrunken. Liver greatly shrunken, firm, grayish brown on the cut surface. Spleen dark red, solidified. Contour of left kidney normal, capsule easily detachable, tracery somewhat effaced. Right kidney dry, dark brown. Stomach empty, mucous membrane a dirty pink, dry. Intestines hardened. Mucous membrane grayish red. Contents typical, somewhat dry. Bladder contracted, mucous membrane gray. During autopsy a marked smell of bitter almonds.

Appended:
1. Wide-mouth test tube containing 6 metal fragments.
2. Test tube with glass fragments from the ampule.

Signatures of the Commission:

Same as on p. 88.

CONCLUSION

Based on the forensic-medical examination of the partially burned corpse of an unknown woman and on reports on other corpses in this group (Documents Nos. 1-11) the Commission reaches the following conclusions:

1. *Anatomical characteristics of the body:*
In view of the fact that the body parts are extensively charred, it is impossible to describe the features of the dead woman.

113

The following, however, could be established:

a) The age of the dead woman lies between 30 and 40 years, evidence of which is also the only slightly worn masticating surface of the teeth;

b) Stature: about 150 cm.;

c) The most important anatomical finding for identification of the person are the gold bridge of the lower jaw and its four front teeth.

2. *Cause of death:*

On the extensively charred corpse there were found traces of a splinter injury to the thorax with hemothorax, injuries to one lung and to the pericardium, as well as six small metal fragments.

Further, remnants of a crushed glass ampule were found in the oral cavity.

In view of the fact that similar ampules were present in other corpses—Documents Nos. 1, 2, 3, 4, 5, 6, 7, 8, 9, 10, 11—that a smell of bitter almonds developed upon dissection—Documents Nos. 1, 2, 3, 4, 5, 6, 7, 8, 9, 10, 11—and based on the forensic-chemical tests of the internal organs of these bodies in which the presence of cyanide compounds was established—Documents Nos. 1, 2, 3, 4, 5, 6, 7, 8, 9, 10, 11—the Commission reaches the conclusion that notwithstanding the severe injuries to the thorax, the immediate cause of death was poisoning by cyanide compounds.

Signatures of the Commission:

Same as on p. 88.